Praise About
"Legends of the Grail"

"An outstanding and beautifully illustrated study."

—Dr Leonee Ormond, Kings College London, England

"If ever someone had found and resurrected the missing half of the Bible, it would be Ayn Cates Sullivan."

—Christina Sophia Stellarum, MDiv. Harvard University

"When women read this they will understand themselves for the first time; when men read this book they will awaken to the exquisite power of women."

—Susan Allan CEO The Marriage Forum, Inc.

"A powerful transmission of the feminine voices of my homeland. Love it!"

—Mara Luasa, Connemara, Ireland

"Ayn Cates Sullivan is masterful in weaving stories that heal as you read them, and this book is no exception.

—Dr Susan Lange, OMD L.Ac., Santa Monica, CA, USA

"Lost have the stories of the female been, often times overshadowed by stories of the man, until now. Reading these stories is like reading a part of my history I never knew."

— Jennifer Chapman Sendzimir, Teacher, Tennesse, USA

Also by Ayn Cates Sullivan, Ph.D.

A Story of Becoming

Three Days in the Light

Sparkle & the Rainbow Dragon

Sparkle & The Light

Sparkle & The Gift

The Windhorse: Poems of Illumination

Consider This: Recovering Harmony & Balance Naturally

Tracking the Deer

egends
of the
Grail

Stories of Celtic Goddesses

AYN CATES SULLIVAN, Ph.D.

Infinite Light Publishing
Santa Barbara, CA

Infinite Light Publishing
5142 Hollister Avenue, No. 115
Santa Barbara, CA 93111
www.infinitelightpublishing.com

First Edition

Library of Congress Control Number: PS3619.U42 L442 2017

Cataloging-in-Publication:

Names: Sullivan, Ayn Cates, author. | DuCray, Belle Crow, illustrator.

Title: *Legends of the Grail: Stories of Celtic Goddesses* / Ayn Cates Sullivan; illustrations by Belle Crow duCray.

Description: First edition. | Santa Barbara, CA: Infinite Light Publishing, [2017] | Includes bibliographical references and index.

Identifiers: ISBN: 978-0-9884537-8-4 (paperback) | 978-0-9970467-1-7 (ebk) | 978-0-9884537-9-1 (hardcover)

Subjects: LCSH: Goddesses, Celtic--Fiction. | Goddesses, Irish--Fiction. | Mythology, Celtic--Fiction. | Mythology, British--Fiction. | Women, Celtic--Folklore. | Women--Folklore. | Magic, Celtic--Fiction. | Nature--Mythology --Fiction. | Families--Fiction. | Determination (Personality trait)--Fiction. | Self-actualization (Psychology)--Fiction. | Spirituality--Fiction. | BISAC: BODY, MIND & SPIRIT. | FICTION / Fairy Tales, Folk Tales, Legends & Mythology. | FAMILY & RELATIONSHIPS. | YOUNG ADULT FICTION / Legends, Myths, Fables. | LITERARY COLLECTIONS. | NATURE. | SELF-HELP.

Summary: If Eve could retell her story, do you think she would share it any differently? *Legends of the Grail, Ireland's Missing Tales* is a collection of Irish myths and legends told in the traditional way, with a twist. Each Goddess (generally demonized or misunderstood) has the chance to retell her story in a way that liberates her from centuries of misunderstanding. Some of the legends date back eight thousand years, yet the wisdom is timeless.

Illustrations: Belle Crow duCray
Editor: Robin Quinn
Book Cover: Lucinda Rae
Graphic Design: Ghislain Viau

These stories are dedicated to my mother,
Gwen Cates, the first Goddess in my life,
an artist who invites me to imagine.
And my father, Bill Cates
Who encourages me
To dream &
tell stories.
May we
never
forget our
origin
of Infinite Light.

Contents

Acknowledgments

From the Sky above
To the Earth below —
Thank you!

A man who has embraced his Divine Feminine is the most delicious of all men! He has emerged from the womb of his mother and then has made the journey of re-birth through the womb of the Goddess within. I want to thank my husband, John Patrick Sullivan, for being an incredible man who can hold space for the Goddess energies emerging within me, while also discovering and surrendering to the deep Celtic feminine aspects arising within his own psyche. Thank you for holding the space so that the healing world of Tir Na Ban and the Land of Women could find its way to me again. I also want to thank all the other men who encourage the re-emergence of the Goddess, including my son, William Mussman. These are the men who can become true partners, beloveds and husbands, for they are finding balance within their own psyches.

Thank you Marcela Benson for studying Kabbalah with me, and helping me make the links between Judaism, Christianity, and Gaelic Ireland. The Tree of Life lives within me now. I am so grateful to you for reminding me that, once we know the stories of the Goddesses, it is then time to live and eat like one. Thank you Marcela for being a wonderful friend and support, without you this book might still be sitting on a dusty shelf.

Thank you to Belle Crow duCray, the amazing and magical illustrator who spent time reading the stories, dreaming, and drawing the Goddesses and Gods in these pages. Thank you for truly bringing *Legends of the Grail* to life!

Much gratitude is extended to my daughter, Kathryn Hamilton, who has spent years walking in sacred places with me collecting folklore. Thank you, Christina Sophia Stellarum, for encouraging me to share these stories in a more public way.

With deep respect, I would like to step back to the beginning of this work to King's College London and thank my mentor, Dr. Leonee Ormond, for helping me obtain an Overseas Research Award so that I could pursue my interest in Celtic Mythology. Although they have long crossed beyond the veil, I also wish to thank the early leaders of the Irish Literary Renaissance, Isabella Augusta Gregory and William Butler Yeats, for inspiring the Irish (and eventually the Western World) to remember the importance of the myths and legends that arise out of the landscape of Ireland and the rest of the British Isles. The Emerald Isles are full of treasures waiting to be rediscovered. I also want to thank my friend from Ireland, Suzanna Crampton, for walking ancient sites with me and exploring the mysteries and for the wonderful day at the Holy Thorn when the sky sent confirmation of the Otherworlds. I extend heartfelt gratitude to the Russian poet, Joseph Brodsky, for reminding me that sharing the voices of mystics can change the world; and to Dr. Andrew St. George for being the role model of a true writer.

My gratitude is extended to Mirabai Devi for being a living example Goddess, and for being daring enough to read the visualization of the "The Cailleach" with me on an online program, literally bringing this ancient Earth Goddess back to life. May we all find the wholesomeness and wisdom of the Cailleach and the ancient ones within ourselves.

I want to acknowledge my brilliant editors, Robin Quinn, Ken Zeiger, and Mcgovren Moore who helped me refine and polish these pages. There are so many people who have supported the emergence of *Legends of the Grail* and have helped this book become a reality. Most of all, thank you, Divine Light, the Sidhe, and the ancient ones for showing me the way in each and every moment.

I wish to express my respect and give gratitude to my book shepherd, Ellen Reid, who crossed beyond the veil during this project. You are missed. May your journey on the Otherside be gentle and blessed.

Academic Foreword

Ayn Cates Sullivan, the author of *Legends of the Grail: Stories of the Celtic Goddesses,* was a postgraduate student under my supervision at King's College, London. She left us with a PhD for an excellent thesis on the life and work of Augusta, Lady Gregory. Together with William Butler Yeats, Lady Gregory played a very important part in the establishment of the Irish Dramatic Movement and of Dublin's famous Abbey Theatre. Gregory herself wrote many plays among them *Cathleen ni Houlihan* (written with Yeats), *Hyacinth Halvey*, and *The Rising of the Moon*.

In her thesis, as in this book, Ayn paid particular attention to the growing interest in Irish folklore and the 'Celtic Revival' in the late nineteenth and early twentieth centuries. Lady Gregory's volumes of folk and mythic material, *Cuchulain of Muirthemne* of 1902, *Gods and Fighting Men* of 1904 and her *Kiltartan Books* of 1909 and 1910, all made a great contribution to this movement and are of relevance to *Legends of the Grail.* Ayn also included in her thesis a pioneering study of Augusta Gregory's translations from Molière, showing the extent to which Gregory cut and reorganised the French dramatist's plays for an Irish audience, and considering the effect of Molière on Gregory's own theory of comedy.

After completing her thesis, Ayn has gone on to a very successful career as a writer. Her published work represents a considerable contribution to the literature of legend and of myth. Her remarkable book for children, *A Story of Becoming* of 2014, has won eighteen literary prizes, with several gold medals amongst them. A young seed begins to grow into an apple tree, but has to contend with many setbacks. If *Legends of the Grail* opens up another world, that of the Celtic goddesses, it also demonstrates the processes of the growth of the spirit, and of the difficulties to be overcome in fulfilling one's destiny.

As Ayn tells us in her Author's note, she herself has Irish forebears, and her study takes in Irish and Scottish legend. Danu, the mother goddess, is, appropriately, the first of seven figures who tell their own story and who are presented in detail. Opening the way for what is to come, with her background in the wider world, Danu is associated here with the landscape, with water, hills, plains and the sea. As Ayn tells us, Danu's daughters, who include Dagda, Brighid, Aine and Eriu, appear in other parts of this book, as does Tir na Ban, the mystical land of women to which Danu and her children make their way.

Ayn also shows how some of these figures can be linked to Judaic and Christian traditions. Anu, another name for Danu, has been associated with St Anne, the grandmother of Jesus. Aine, the solar goddess, and a daughter of Danu, was also incorporated into Christian worship as St Anne. Brighid, whose legend goes back for fifteen thousand years, has been incorporated into the Irish Christian church as the fifth to sixth century nun St Brigid, who was associated with St Patrick, and is a patron saint of Ireland. She is also the subject of a play by Lady Gregory, *The Story Brought by Brigit* of 1924, in which she is present at the crucifixion of Christ.

Most striking of all in this respect is the legend of Ayn's second goddess, Ceasair, the grand-daughter of Noah, who, like her grandfather, set sail in order to escape from the danger of the flood. Descended from Cain rather than Abel, she is unable to travel with her grandfather, but, guided and protected by another of the Irish goddesses, Eriu, her party goes first to Spain, and then on to Bantry Bay, where they land and then go on to settle in Ireland. Several of the goddesses are, like Danu, associated with particular places in Ireland and with rivers and hills. The reference to specific locations, whether in Ireland or in Western Scotland, takes in a number of well-known sites, including Skye, Knockainey, the Hill of Tara, Dun Aengus and the River Boyne. "Mythology is a sacred part of the living landscape," Ayn tells us, and she adds that Coole Park, home of Lady Gregory is amongst the places which have influenced her own writing career.

Each of the goddesses speaks for herself, in a separate section following the account of a particular figure. Their voices are heard, and readers are encouraged to experience them, often in relation to the natural world, or to the Irish or Scottish landscape. We, as readers, can live more fully if we enter into this relationship with a controlling and absorbing force.

This is a book which concentrates on sacred women, but they are often seen in relation to their male relatives, fathers, husbands, lovers and sons. Caer loves the poet Aengus who first sees her as a swan. Emer marries the legendary hero Cucuhulain, who already has a child by the warrior goddess Scatach, and they have three daughters. (Yeats took on another aspect of the relationship of these two legendary figures in his play *The Only Jealousy of Emer* of 1919).

Legends *of the Grail* shows us into an ancient world, which has parallels and influences in our own day. We learn about the colours and the plants and trees associated with particular goddesses, and also about the objects, for example the cauldron or the churn, which are part of their legends. The list of names and terms at the end of the book is invaluable and even tells us how to pronounce them.

I cannot help thinking that the subject of Ayn's thesis, Augusta Gregory, would be delighted, and fascinated, by this outstanding and beautifully illustrated study.

Dr Leonee Ormond
Professor of Literature
King's College London

Foreword
Inspiring Women of the Land

I have known Ayn Cates Sullivan for over 30 years. We met when we were both wild young nymphs stretching our wings full of adventure. Over the years our bodies and minds have matured, and yet we still take delight in exploring and discovering who we are today. We have shared many adventures and explorations in both England and Ireland, finding hidden gems of ancient mythological history in the lands of our ancestors. I was honored that Ayn asked me to write the forward to her new book.

Legends of the Grail: Stories of Celtic Goddesses is a book of Irish Goddesses, their stories, myths and legends. Not only is this book full of the history of fascinating Irish Goddesses and their stories, it also includes blessings and poems capturing their essence. There are written meditations and visualizations which, if followed, will help the reader become more aware of the environment and one's self, especially in relationship to the natural world. Reading these stories is a wonderful way to help inspire women, and men, to find their own Goddess within.

Reading the book reminds me of the early days, when I first met Ayn. The meeting was a bit of a surprise. Ayn returned home from university unexpectedly, not knowing her parents were away, or that I had been employed as the house and farm sitter. It was clear from the start that we were both free-spirited, and rather undomesticated. We prowled around each other like a pair of cornered cats ready to strike out with verbal claw or fang. We both managed to contain our feral selves and formed a tempered friendship of convenience as we lived for a week together in her parent's house. Years went by and our paths crossed multiple times.

One occasion comes vividly to mind of a New Year's Day party a friend and I were throwing under the shadows of the Blue Ridge Mountains. On the cabin's back porch with a view of the mountains in their indigo blue, I introduced two dear friends who were both pregnant for the first time. One was local to Charlottesville, Virginia. The other was Ayn, who was living in London, England at the time. Both women briefly stroked each other's beautiful bellies, which were ripening for birth in the coming year. Both women spoke of impending Motherhood, heads bowed. Each had a hand on the other's belly as they talked about their first-born. Whether they were going to have a boy or girl was unknown to both. I stood in the cabin's doorway looking out on this scene of these two female friends, silhouetted by the bright sun and with the mountains of Virginia glorious in their rich blue hue. This was the only time these two women met and talked, yet both had their daughters within hours, if not minutes, of each other. The names of their daughters are remarkably similar. One was named Hannah Catherine, and the other Kathryn Ayn.

Living in Ireland as a woman farmer with a flock of sheep has taught me that there is a history of misogyny amongst the farming community that still endures. In response, I helped start a support group for women farmers called "Women of the Land." Our local group is called "South East Women in Farming, Ireland," or SEWFI. As we were deciding on a logo for our group, I felt it should be a universal emblem of agriculture. Remembering Aine, the Irish Goddess of grains, grasses and early agriculture, I came up with a logo depicting sheaves of grain draped in the shape of a women's eyebrow. I continue to encourage women to step up beyond the role of unpaid book keeper, calf feeder, or the one who stands in the gap to keep a flock or herd on a chosen path. I still urge women of the land to take ownership of the honorable title "Farmer."

One day I was asked to give an inspirational talk to our female farming group in order to help the women in my community find courage and a feeling of pride as farmers. To encourage them, I spoke about the history and evolution of agriculture. I reminded them that once we were tribes roaming the land, hunting and gathering in the wilds of nature. The men were often hunters, while the women with children gathered grains, fruits, nut and roots. It occurred to me that there were certainly women whose gathering skills influenced the way we tend domesticated animals today. Orphaned lambs follow whoever gives them a sup of milk, and this has not changed through the ages.

Imagine for a moment that we are in the era of hunters and gathers. There is a breast-feeding shepherd who comes across an orphaned wild sheep or goat. With instinctive generosity, she shares her breast-milk with the lamb or kid. This young animal then follows the tribe of women gatherers. As women move from location to location, they collect more animals, which are tended and harvested accordingly. The women, still gathering and hunting, would have become shepherds to a small herd or flock of animals which followed them and began to depend upon these early keepers of domesticated livestock. Shepherds would eventually have observed that where animals had left behind their manure, grass would grow richer, greener and sweeter. So why not drop some seeds of grain in the soil near the manure? These early shepherds would return to find stronger bigger grains growing. Being a *"Farm – Her"* is in our blood, in our souls and engrained within us as women.

The Roman Goddess of grain is known as Ceres, which is where we get the name *"cereals,"* an agricultural term for most grains now grown by modern farmers. The Irish equivalent of Ceres is Aine, the Goddess of grains and grasses, a mighty woman who appears in this book. One of the better known Irish Goddess is Brighid, Goddess of water, spring, fertility and healing. She is spoken of as the Goddess whom poets adore. The Goddesses in this book can encourage "Women of the Land" to own their strengths and to come out from behind the farm door. Brighid's tale appears in the last story of this book, "Brighid's Search for the Cailleach." Ayn writes these stories with an ease that encourages the reader to find one's inner strength, to bare witness to one's own life and lay claim to one's path.

Suzanna Crampton
Irish Famer
Maiden Hall
Kilkenny, Ireland

Author's Note
Discovering My Irish Ancestry

When I was growing up in Virginia, I was very fortunate because both sets of my grandparents were still alive, and I was able to learn about my ancestors and their origins. When you discover where the clay of your body is from, it is sometimes possible to become more acquainted with your soul. If you listen carefully you may hear the whispers of those who still live within you, because they loved enough to dream you into being.

I loved hearing stories about my great-great-grandfather on my mother's side who had emigrated from England and was buried with his brother, on my grandparents' farm in Virginia, which is still in the family. I am not certain if the story is true, but my imagination loves the idea. My research indicates that a line of Foster ancestry goes back to the Forrester warriors of Bamburgh Castle in Northumbria. An early Forrester Bible verifies that our lineage is Scottish nobility that links back to ancient Ireland and the Irish King Niall of the Nine Hostages, the father of the Ui Neill Family. It seemed to me, even as a child, that my true home was far away, in a land that was green and magical.

My father's grandfather, who enjoyed fishing and spending time reflecting by the water, blamed his fluctuating moods on his Irish heritage. Perhaps he was called to go out to the water's edge because, like his ancestors, he could hear the Salmon of Wisdom whispering to him.

Many years later when I met the man who was to be my true beloved and husband, John Patrick Sullivan, one of the first things I said to him was, "I know your lineage. You are a descendent of the Munster Kings of Ireland!"

An Overseas Research Award

In 1985, I was offered an overseas research award from King's College London to research the life and work of Lady Gregory. I had never heard of her, but I was familiar with her contemporary, William Butler Yeats, and eager to earn my doctorate in Anglo-Irish Literature. I knew that Yeats had been obsessed with the mysticism of Ireland, and after I made the journey to the west of Ireland, I began to understand why.

The flight from London to Dublin is short, but the trip to County Galway is like going back into time. The former home of Lady Gregory, Coole Park, is located near the town of Gort, in the west of Ireland. Coole Park is now a thousand-acre nature reserve. A large Beech tree, known as the autograph tree, grows in a walled garden bearing the names of the writers of the Irish Literary Renaissance.

Isabella Augusta Gregory was a folklorist and dramatist, who co-founded the Abbey Theatre in Dublin. Although she was born into a class that believed in British rule, Lady Gregory became interested in the Irish language and wrote a number of books on Irish myth and folklore, including *Cuchulain of Muirthemne*. After developing a nationalist perspective, Lady Gregory was supportive of introducing the Irish language back into schools. W.B. Yeats felt that her folklore was the best to come out of Ireland. Lady Gregory challenged the illustrious scholars at Trinity College in Dublin, declaring that Irish mythology was as relevant as Greek and Roman myth.

My Experience in the Seven Woods of Coole, Galway, Ireland

Like Yeats, I walked through the seven woods of Coole Park to the place where the wild swans gather in the autumn. Turloughs are lakes that flood during the winter and then dry up during the summer months. Rumor has it that they are connected with the Faery-folk. I had the chance to sit beside a low-lying turlough where Yeats had written his poem, "The Wild Swans at Coole."

I decided to meditate on the sounds the trees made as the branches rubbed together in the wild Atlantic winds. I imagined that I was sitting there with Lady Gregory who was telling me of Emer, the wife of the hero Cuchulain, and the Warrior Goddess Scatach. Lady Gregory liked strong women who chose life over death.

At the time I thought that folklore and myth were just stories made up by people with good imaginations, which in a sense they are. But as I rested at the water's edge, it seemed to me that there was a shimmering girl who walked past. I shook my head and read Yeats' poem, "The Song of Wandering Aengus."

While I read, the trees blew strongly in the wind, and I thought perhaps I should find my way back to the car. The reeds around the shimmering water seemed to wave in such a way that I began to wonder if perhaps I was being invited into a secret world. As I contemplated Yeats' silver apples of the moon and the golden apples of the sun, the first draft of Caer's story came to me.

I realized sitting there that the landscape was alive with legends, and I began to wonder if there is in fact a mystical dimension that exists just beyond the human senses.

Searching for the Goddess

The Long Room Library at Trinity College holds many of Ireland's treasures, including a manuscript known as the *Book of Kells*. In the dimly lit corridor, I marveled at the many literary treasures. I saw the marble busts of great white male philosophers, thinkers and writers. Even most of the myths and folklore I had read at that time were about heroes, not heroines. I wondered how I fit into all of it. Was I going to be overlooked like most female writers and poets? Even Lady Gregory was largely forgotten after her death and her plays rarely performed.

I needed a role model, and since there were few I could study, I decided to reach back in time and research Goddesses to discover more about the true essence of the feminine. It seemed to me that the best place to begin was walking amongst the cairns, stone circles and passage tombs of Ireland. The more time I spent walking on sacred sites, the more I realized there are stories that are etched into the land. If we listen quietly amongst the ancient stones, or by the edge of a lake or ocean, we can hear the ancient ones sharing tales, even now. Mythology is a sacred part of the living landscape.

Introduction
The Legends of the Grail Stories

Legends of the Grail is a series of books that include the Goddesses of Ireland and Britain. This volume contains seven short stories that arise out of the landscape of Ireland, as well as some other whimsical tales that are scattered throughout the book. The word "Celtic" is used in this book when referring to a larger landscape and the mythologies of Northwestern Europe, Britain, and Ireland.

In each chapter, you will find background in the form of a myth or legend traditionally told about each Deity. The myths & legends sections have a header illustration portraying dragons, symbols of the ancient Goddess. Then a story is conveyed from the perspective of each Goddess, usually told in the first person. The Goddess stories often begins with the word "Speaks" and have headers with nine black butterflies, suggesting that the stories hold the potential for transformation.

Realm of the Goddess, Tir Na Ban

In Celtic mythology there is a realm, or parallel dimension of reality, that nurtures feminine impulses. Some call it Avalon while others use the more ancient name of Tir Na Ban (or Tir Na mBan). Also known as the Land of Women, Tir Na Ban is seen by poets as a mystical floating island. Perhaps it is the etheric blueprint of the Goddess that hovers in another dimension over Ireland, England, Scotland, and Wales, and perhaps extending into France. Tir Na Ban is a spiritual Avalon, where Goddesses, Heroines, Faery-folk and Ladies of the Lake reside. Occasionally, their friends and lovers can also visit this magical land.

It is possible to meet the Goddess when meditating beside sacred wells and ancient trees. Throughout the world, mystics know of the Land of the Goddess. The mythologies of other cultures refer to Venusberg, Wonderland, the Hesperides, or Summerland. In Tir Na Ban, it is always springtime and the trees shimmer like polished gemstones. The pure, flowing streams taste like rosewater, and the air is always perfumed with the scent of blossoming flowers. The Earth in Tir Na Ban is honored and protected in the ancient ways of the Goddess. Wild swans, songbirds and butterflies know how to slip through the veils. If your heart is open and pure, perhaps you, too, may be treated to a glimpse.

Healing with the Goddess

After the retelling of each legend, a Goddess is specifically honored, including the time of the year in which she can be celebrated. The plants, flowers, animals, and/or familiars that are considered sacred to her also are listed. When we know what aspects of nature are connected with a Goddess it is easier for us to connect to her essence in the living world.

The world is alive with color. In each chapter you will discover three sacred colors that I feel are attuned to the essence of each

Goddess, as well as the esoteric meaning behind the colors. Three is the number of the triple Goddess, and it is a way women have of artistically expressing themselves. It is a light-hearted invitation to notice, embrace, and then include the essence of color and learn more about our selves in the process. In the pages that follow, we discover the soul qualities and capacities of each Goddess and how they may impact us. Finally, we are invited to engage in practices and visualizations designed to awaken the Goddess within each one of us.

The Goddess Danu safeguards the luminous cup, cauldron or grail, the potent feminine mystery out of which all things arise. When necessary, the Goddess can become a beacon of Light throughout all time and can empower others, like Cuchulain, to become a hero or heroine. The practices and visualizations at the end of each chapter help us recall our inner light, trust our destiny, and discover our true power.

Words have paths and destinies. The language used in the visualizations is meant to take you on a Quest to meet an archetype, deity or Goddess, and also to a gift of understanding that is awaiting you. The practices of quieting the mind, walking in nature, and meditation, as well as the visualizations, teach us how to become receptive and how to navigate the spiritual dimensions. Blessings are a way we have of reaching into the flame of True Nature, and bringing light to this world.

When we link to the energy of a Goddess in a story or visualization, it can be deeply soothing, or even quite emotional. Allow yourself to simply be with the feelings that arise. Many of the Goddesses in this book were misunderstood, and when they re-tell their stories, you may also become aware that you might like to tell the tales of your life in a more enlightened way. When you speak, remember that you are uttering sounds that bring life into manifestation. These are healing stories that can help us on the Quest to the discovery of the Grail, or our True Nature.

Men and women, who are in touch with their inner Goddesses, understand how to be embodied, and can live like kings and queens on Earth. Before journeying to the Otherworlds, take time to prepare yourself and create a sacred space.

You might wish to find or design a special garden or sanctuary where you will not be disturbed. If you prefer to be indoors, it is easy to place a chair in a quiet room and close the door. You can elaborate by creating altars using the flowers, leaves, symbols, and colors of the Goddesses. Dressing in soft and colorful clothing, putting essential oils on your skin, sipping gem elixirs, and designing a pleasant sanctuary for yourself is part of the practice of remembering and embodying the Goddesses.

Once you feel satisfied that your sacred space is right for you, find a comfortable position, close your eyes and take three deep breaths. Three is the number sacred to the Goddess and it helps you enter Her dimension. Open up, and receive the gentle and nurturing energies of the Goddesses. Allow this river of light to heal your body, mind, and soul, so that you feel whole again.

Blessings

At the end of each section you will find a blessing from each Goddess designed to help you remember an aspect of your own light. A blessing is a spark of light that can only share its gifts when someone receives it. A spark by its nature removes all darkness, in the same way that the darkness vanishes when we turn on the light in a room. Danu knew that she had to hide her inner light until it was time for the blessings of her children to be shared again. Like Noah, Ceasair listened to her guidance and threw the light of her heart out into the future, trusting that her wish for a good life would be answered. Eriu heard her call and welcomed her to the emerald isle. May you also be blessed and find your way to truth, love, health and wisdom.

The Appendices, Glossary & Bibliography

There are several Appendices at the end of the book. "Appendix I – Pantheon of Celtic Divinities" is a useful reference for the complex relationships of the Deities found in these stories. "Appendix II – *Lebor Gabala Erenn's* – Six Invasions of Ireland" lists the timeline of the early history of Ireland, now thought to be a pseudo history or myth. "Appendix III – A Goddess Timeline and 'Thealogy': *Her-story*" is a historical and intuitive guideline of the formation of the Earth and human civilization from a feminine perspective. "Appendix IV – Calendar of the Goddess: *Balanced Sun & Moon*," is an eight wheel calendar showing eight ancient holidays, still used by Neo-Pagans, that follow natural cycles of the Sun and Moon.

Gaelic names may seem complicated at first, but at the back of the book, you will find a Glossary to help you with pronunciation, as well as a brief dictionary of Irish myth and legend. If you wish to learn more about Irish Mythology, I have provided a lengthy Bibliography.

Harp, Club & Cauldron
The Three Treasures of Ireland

T he High King of the Tuatha Dé Danann, the Dagda, possessed three treasures: a harp that put the seasons in order, a magical club that could kill nine men with one blow, and a special cauldron known as Undry, or in Irish, *Coire Unsic*. As a father figure, the Dagda was revered as a fertile Earth-God and venerated by those who wished to live in right alignment with life. In Irish mythology, the Dagda's Cauldron of Bounty and Abundance was made by a Druid named Semias in a city called Murias, far to the north. The *Coire Unsic* was known as a source of everlasting nourishment, life, bounty, and abundance, because when this vessel was placed on a fire, no one would leave it unsatisfied.

The Cauldron appears later in history as a Grail, Chalice, or Cup of Christ, and they are all feminine symbols. Although the Cauldron can sometimes be dismissed as a cooking vessel, the ancient people honored the Cauldron of Bounty and Abundance. They knew that their survival was dependent upon the fertility of the land. The wise Dagda understood that no male Deity could ever possess the Cauldron, any more than he could possess a woman of Tir Na Ban, but he could be its guardian and protector. He safeguarded *Coire Unsic* as the sacred womb, a source of both nurturing and life.

DANU

Danu in Celtic
Myth & Legend
The Great Mother Goddess

There was once a time when every well, spring, and river was considered a sacred portal to the Goddess. The erudite say that we find wisdom at the water's edge, and it is there that spiritual illumination is given. Calling upon the Goddess on our Grail quest requires emptying ourselves of what we are not and being humble enough to discover the truth of who we are. It is not for the faint of heart, but it is a quest for seekers of truth.

Danu was the name of the Mother Goddess of the early inhabitants of Ireland. She is an ancient, Indo-European Mother Goddess who bestows life and abundance. Although only a few myths about Danu still exist, there are many places that bear her name. Some scholars and poets say that she arose from the River Danube in Eastern Europe. Others claim that she still resides in the Paps of Anu in Ireland, two breast-shaped hills that were capped with stones like nipples. Danu can be seen as an ever-flowing river of Otherworldly grace. It may be that she is as ancient as the Earth itself.

Perhaps the reason the Goddess traditions were oppressed was because both men and women knew intuitively that, at some point, they would be required to pass through the womb of the Great Mother again in death. Refusing to surrender, we became warriors and did everything we could to stop the inevitable change. However, there is more wisdom in understanding that we change and our bodies transform, perhaps even into light. Today, we can still visit the ancient passage tombs (or passage wombs) such as Newgrange or Loughcrew and feel the way in which the All Mother holds us. It is an eternal embrace.

In Irish mythology, Danu partnered with Bilé (meaning "sacred tree"), the Celtic God of Light and Healing. Danu and her children are linked to goodness and the fertility of the land. Their son, the good Dagda, was the original leader of the Tuatha Dé Danann. Many of Danu's daughters will emerge in the chapters of this book.

Danu, the All Mother Goddess, appears throughout Celtic myths and legends. In Welsh mythology, she is known as Don and in Sanskrit as Dana (meaning "waters of heaven"). Danu is also linked with the Greek Mother Goddess, Demeter. Anu or Ana is another name for Danu, sometimes appearing as a sister. The Goddess Aine is generally considered to be her daughter. They were both eventually absorbed into Christianity as Saint Anne, the grandmother of Jesus, to whom many holy wells are dedicated. In Glamorgan, South Wales, Saint Anne's ancient link to Anu is depicted in a fountain with water gushing from her nipples. Danu has a long history of divine light and goodness.

Danu's earliest stories arise out of the mythology of Ireland's Divine race, the Tuatha Dé Danann, or Sidhe, whom poets say travelled from Greece to Ireland during the Bronze Age, around 3000 BC. Other mystics claim these wise beings travelled from the stars. Over time, their status was diminished from Divinities to Faery-folk, or even corrupted into frightening stories such as "Black Annis of Britain"—a tale about a witch who was reputed to steal little children and eat them. However, as Celtic mythology is restored and increasingly honored, we find that the Tuatha Dé Danann include many notable Deities such as Brighid (who became known as Bride, Brigid and eventually Saint Brigit), as well as Eriu, another Mother Goddess of Ireland.

Throughout mythology, Danu is the great mystery—the Goddess of the primordial waters of creation. She appears in every culture as the principal of birth and beginning, the one who loves and understands us. She is both light and darkness; the one who gives us life and later reclaims us through death. Danu enfolds us in velvety darkness and also warms us with the rays of her light. She is as warm as the sun shining on the ocean, and as cold as the stones in a winter river. Danu is as old as time and as young as each breath. Her name is known everywhere but her face is largely unseen.

Danu is both transcendent and embodied, reminding us how we can embrace our true feminine attributes, such as love, compassion and understanding. Constantly changing, growing, discovering, and evolving, we begin to understand our True Nature. When Danu comes to us as a guide, we learn that we can embrace all aspects of ourselves (the good, bad and ugly) with love and acceptance. Her energy is that of a sacred river, cleansing and restoring all facets of our being so that we shine like polished crystals and gemstones.

The Cosmic Mother force helps us understand and comprehend life. When we are aligned with the Mother our thinking becomes peaceful, our speech has clarity, and our actions have purpose. With the trinity of thought, speech and action in balance, we have the possibility to create the Kingdom (or Queendom) in which goodness can dwell. Sometimes we are required to take a journey deep inside until the right time arises for the gifts that we bring. Danu has been waiting for thousands of years, and yet she understands that the once and future King and Queen will hold hands on Earth once again.

Danu Speaks
Ireland's Missing Tale

The coming of the warring Milesians made it clear that the period of three thousand years of peace, beauty, abundance, and song had ended. We had completed our cycle. We gathered our tribe and spoke with as much wisdom as we could about the events that must occur. We had come from the Otherworlds and had nurtured the land until all upon it blossomed—but things change.

I will never forget Fand, that little pearl of beauty, sobbing as she made her way into the Otherworlds through *Ceis Churainn*, the caves of Keshcorran. She could not understand why we must disappear from the sight and memory of men. I think it was her love for the great hero Cuchulain that made her suffer so. She did not want to leave him behind. But the great Sea God, Manannan Mac Lir, guided her safely under the waves to Tir Na Ban, the Land of Women.

That day, I stood with my son, the good Dagda, and we looked across the fine fields and valleys of Ireland, remembering our lives there. I glanced at him and saw a tear running down his right cheek. Perhaps he feared that goodness would leave the surface Earth with

21

him. Certainly, his benevolence and laughter sustained us as we went to our new kingdom.

We don't age quickly, like humans, for we are of a more ancient race and have the knowledge of regeneration. We do love humankind, yet we do not respect the ways of domination and violence. That is why we wept, and also why we departed from the land we love. I knew, as I looked around us, that a difficult time was coming for humanity and Earth. There would be wars and famines, tears and bloodshed. My daughters—Badb, Macha, and Nemain—were warriors who fought for the Tuatha and what they believed in. I had wished for peace, but there are tides and cycles larger than we are, and we had to simply abide by them. Eventually, my fierce daughters grew weary and joined us beneath the waves.

My name is Danu and I am known as the Great Mother Goddess of Goodness and Light. When I came from the stars, we still had the ability to reproduce by thought. Some children came from my womb, but others, like Flidais, were born out of the trees. Boann arose from a river, but the Dagda and Eriu came from within me. It was a magical time, before the world became dense and filled with smoke and fire.

I do not understand the race of men, so I have largely withdrawn into wells and lakes, deep inside the earth. I can take on a form, and have come back to men and women. Sometimes I visit in the shape of a wolf or dog, or stand quietly in the corner of a sacred grove in the form of a Beech tree, or bloom in your garden as a fragrant rose. I taught one of the Ladies of the Lake to breathe beneath the waves and empower kings. Yet my role is not one that fosters war, for I sustain life.

It is true that, sometimes, we must defend ourselves, but the Tuatha Dé Danann chose to live by becoming less dense. It required a shift in consciousness for our entire tribe. Those who had negative feelings could not come with us, but had to mingle in the world of warriors. They were still magical, but their lives were shortened and they were often misunderstood.

It was a violent time and I took many of my daughters with me because I feared for their safety. Brighid and Aine remained above ground, for they found kinship in the Celtic church and were referred to, in time, as saints. Eventually, they also grew tired of persecution and came back to the Sidhe.

It is true that my daughter, Brighid, was a wonderful healer of hearts and bodies. She possessed a special gift, which did cause some alarm amongst mortals. When Brighid was a child, she had the ability to create sunbeams and moonbeams in the palms of her hands. Although she was a poet and good at tending fires, I do believe that her inner warmth was why she was so loved. She was also beautiful, but was particularly fond of eyes. Brighid had an odd habit of pulling her eyes out and adjusting them in some way and then casually placing them back into their sockets. She used to laugh and say that was how she chased away suitors. I assure you, her eyesight was perfect, for she had the gift of regeneration. Unlike my wild daughter, Flidais, Brighid did not want men to pursue her. She was lovely but fiercely independent. Alas, she did have one son named Ruadan who was killed. Ah, she did grieve, but the art of keening is a story for another time. I have grown weary of tales of suffering and woe.

When we went underground, we found that our bodies became lighter. Over time, we were no longer dense, but could move in our light bodies through earth, sky, and sea at will. Even the rays of the sun no longer seemed to penetrate us in the same ways. This shift required new talents. We still had to teach our young on the misty isles and in deep, earthen mounds and tunnels of Tir Na Ban and Tir Na n-og, the Land of Eternal Youth. We eventually grew so light that we could move between the veils of our world and yours without being noticed. Sometimes, we watch human activities, but battles rarely interest us. Mostly we like the wild places, staying near the animals, elementals and spirit beings that live almost silently.

I have come back to you today with a message of hope and life. I want you to be aware that a time could come in which certain humans and other creatures may learn to shift dimensions at will. These are the ways of the Goddess, for no one is ever lost. When you align with life, many things are possible. Technology both helps and threatens us. We must never forget that we are creator beings. We are not as dependent on the material things of Earth as some might want us to believe, and yet we must remember that life is a gift. By learning to align with life, we can have all our needs met in simple and safe ways. We feel that it is possible for human beings to do the same. When you are ready, you can call on one of the Tuatha to be a co-walker with you, so you can learn the mystical ways. Our wish for you is that you learn to carve a round table and understand how to dwell in wisdom and understanding unified with all sentient beings on Earth.

I encourage you to take time in Nature. Plant seeds and flowers in my name, so that you can begin to remember Tir Na Ban and those who have become but folklore on the surface land. Go and listen to the sounds of flowing rivers, the breeze as it combs the leaves of trees, and the birds, crickets, and frogs welcoming dawn and dusk.

The job of human beings and the Tuatha Dé Danann is that of stewardship of our Earth. It is time that we learned to be gentle with each other, to love ourselves, and to love all creation, working with its intelligence and majesty. The Earth is ancient; when you walk upon her, remember to pour your love into her.

I say to you that there are many dimensions, many portals through which you may travel and live. It does require leaving sorrow behind like a worn-out history book. Drop the history of humankind now—all the deeds and misdeeds of others—into my watery lap and step across my hearth as a bright and shining diamond, into a new time.

I am Danu, the Mother Goddess of the Tuatha Dé Danann. I am also your mother, as you call to me. Thank you for allowing me to tell this tale that is at once ancient and modern. I want you to know that the time of the Goddess's return has come. When you utter my name with love in your heart and peace in your mind, I will come to you. Even now, I hold you in my arms, which are as vast as the Paps of Anu. My arms have become rivers, my body wide as continents, and my soul one with the sea. I can also come to you as a woman who loves you and in whom there is deep, abiding trust. Relax into my deep embrace and feel the song that flows to you now from the silence of an ancient past …

Healing with Danu

Finding Danu
Maiden, Mother, & Wise Woman

As an archetype Danu is the embodiment of the understanding and nurturing mother archetype. She is patient and enduring, staying with us from our birth, throughout our lives, and even in our crossing to the Otherside of the veil. We can relax into the vast embrace of the Great Mother, for she will carry us throughout eternity. When we look for her, we discover more about our true feminine qualities and capacities.

Danu is traditionally celebrated on January 18 (Day of Danu), as the wise Great Mother Goddess who shows us the way, as well as on March 9 (Mother Goddess Day). The early Irish honored the role of the human mother, and festivals honoring the Great Mother may go back six thousand years or farther. On March 9, small dolls or statues of the Mother Goddess are created to adorn the house. Danu is also celebrated in the springtime on May 1, as a May Queen during the festival of Beltane, one of the four great festivals of the Celtic year. Each of her three celebration days represents a different aspect of Danu: In January, she is the Wise Woman; in March, she is the fertile Mother; and on Beltane, she is the Maiden or May Queen. She also reminds us that time is not linear, but instead a spiral that connects the past, present and future, which exist in the heart of the Goddess as the present moment.

One gentle way to celebrate Danu is to walk around a sacred body of water, such as a well or urn filled with water. As you walk, remember the Great Mother Goddess and how she supports your Quest. You may notice a tree, animal, or color aligned with the Goddess, which is a sign that she is with you.

Danu in Nature
Queen of Moons & Beech Trees

For the Great Goddess, the year is made up of thirteen, twenty-eight-day Moon cycles, which in turn are linked to women's monthly fertility cycles. On the journey to remembering our wholeness, we will notice that the phases of the Moon and the whispers of the trees help us re-establish a rhythm with our own True Nature.

Each month, we can see the three faces of Danu. During the waxing Moon, when the lit section is growing and energies building, we can recognize the youthful maiden aspect of the Goddess. At the time of the full Moon, when the energies and light are at their peak, we recognize Danu as the Mother Goddess. As the energies disperse and the lit portion decreases, under the waning Moon, we come to know the Crone or Wise Woman.

When we live in alignment with the phases of the Moon, we become increasingly aware of how all aspects of the Goddess live within us and within all of Nature. One of Danu's mystical and life-affirming symbols is the Uroboros, the dragon or serpent eating its own tail, reminding us of the infinite intelligence that pervades the universe.

Both ancient and modern Druids honor Nature and listen to the wisdom that the trees, animals, birds, fish, reptiles, and insects have to share. This is important because they are all an integral part of existence. Danu's special animal is the Wolf, whose medicine is to awaken the teacher within us.

29

Danu's name in Ogham on her Beech Tree

Beech Queen

Each tree in this book contains a deva or spirit, which is closely linked with one of the Goddesses. Danu's sacred tree is the graceful Beech. The bark of the Beech was used to make the first books, and so the tree is associated with the written word. Although Beech trees are not native to Ireland, they play an important role in myth and legend.

Oghma, the son of the good Dagda and grandson of Danu, is said to have created an early Irish writing known as Ogham, or the Celtic Tree Alphabet. Scholars agree that Ogham was used in the 3rd century until the 6th century when it was replaced with the Roman alphabet. There are several early manuscripts that claim that Ogham and Gaelic are ancient languages created soon after the Tower of Babel. There are twenty characters in Ogham, and it is read from the roots of the tree skyward, it also appears on some standing stones. Since Beech trees are trees known to inspire writing, it is fitting to begin this book by honoring one of these great trees.

Not only is the Beech known as the writing tree, but also as the Mother Tree of the Woods. As a flower essence, Beech is used to help people see what is good and beautiful in the world around them. When wishing to learn about the wisdom of the Earth, Beechnuts can be used as talismans or charms. In some legends the energetic partner of the Mother Beech is the Oak King.

Danu's Colors
Luminous Black, Green, and Blue

Danu's sacred colors are Luminous Black, Green, and Blue. Three is a number that is sacred to the Goddess, and these colors symbolize various parts of her essence. Like the beginning of the Celtic New Year, Danu arises out of the Luminous Black void to help us remember our potential and power. Like small seeds, we await the signal to begin our personal growth. Green, the color of plant life and the compassionate heart, reminds us to listen to the natural world, for the forest whispers secrets to those ready to hear. Blue invites us to be as open and receptive as the sky, for then the Divine can touch us and take us on journeys beyond our wildest imagination.

This Triple Color combination is called "The Dreaming Earth." Danu's colors invite us to stay attuned to the vast potential that resides within us and encourage us to live our dreams. Those who approach the Quest with a pure heart are the ones who become Grail Champions—for the heart is already enlightened.

Meeting the Goddess Danu

Meeting the Goddesses in this book requires the willingness to enter into the realms of the imagination, where we can meet each one and sip from her Grail. The Goddess is open to the flow of life, which is why her symbol of the Grail has an open top or removable lid. She accepts all aspects of life, no matter how strange they may seem. When you call upon the Great Goddess Danu, you might encounter an extraordinary loving presence.

To meet Danu, gaze into the nighttime sky and feel the presence that pervades the universe. The black spaciousness that exists in the potency between stars can free your mind from its concerns and limitations. Close your eyes and enter the void now. Surrender all pain, suffering, and agitation. It is in the deep silence that the All Mother Goddess Danu can enter your imagination. Empty yourself totally, so that your mind, heart, and body become receptive and filled with peace.

You were breathed into existence by the play of the void and the light. Sometimes when you silently contemplate Danu, you may smell the scent of flowers, or even taste ambrosia or sweet nectar in your mouth. You may hear gentle music or simply know that there is a presence that has always loved you and will always love you. Allow yourself to imagine a Goddess of Radiant Light.

Practice
Observing Nature

To find Danu, spend time in Nature at night. Pass the night in the open air if you are able, or simply take a chair into your backyard and shift your focus to the nighttime sky. Notice the luminous darkness and observe the many twinkling stars and the visible planets. You may become aware of the planetary zodiac, the three stars in Orion's Belt, or the Big Dipper, so loved by children. If you have a poetic imagination, you might be able to slip through the spaces between stars.

Under the nighttime sky, give thanks for the life that you have been given, for the loving intelligence that fills all sentient beings. Take a few breaths and feel the starlight touching you, guiding you toward your destiny and even greater light.

Visualizatiort
Entering Tir Na Ban,
The Land of Women

The Sun that shines above surface Earth is only one of many suns. Find a safe and comfortable position where you will not be disturbed, then place your hands on your belly and take three deep breaths. Turning your focus downwards, with your inner eye look down into the now translucent soil and imagine that there is a central Sun radiating from the core of the Earth. It is inviting you to explore the mysteries of the Earth. Notice that it is safe and easy to slip out of your body and travel with your Light Body into other dimensions. Ask the Divine Light to protect and safely guide you as your make your way to Tir Na Ban, the Land of Women.

A mysterious light draws you to a sacred part of the landscape. Notice that there are standing stones all around you, and as you walk toward the Light the path becomes increasingly narrow. Squeezing through ancient stones, you find yourself at the entrance of a cairn (or stack of stones). Feeling invited into the cairn, you walk along a tunnel lit with torches. Eventually you find yourself deep inside the cairn, where there are three circular rooms in the shape of a three-leaf clover. In each of the three rooms there is a stone seat. Explore the rooms in a clockwise direction, following the movement and direction of the sun.

First visit the healing seat on the right side of the cairn. As you sit, notice that another world opens up to you. Perhaps you can hear music and feel the warming rays of the ancient ones. It maybe time for something that no longer serves you to pass away into the stones for recycling. It may be an ache in your body or a story of suffering. Allow the ancient ones to recycle what you no longer need.

Feeling lighter you stand up and then walk clockwise to the central room. Sit once again in on a healing stone. This is the place where new awareness may emerge, or perhaps access to the ancient wisdom of the Goddess. Receive your gift of fire or insight with gratitude, and allow it to light up some aspect of your body/mind.

When you are ready walk clockwise to the third and final circular room with another healing seat made of stone. This is where you have the opportunity to integrate what has been released, and the gift that has been received in its place. You may experience a feeling of wholesomeness. Feel the sensations that arise within your body as you stand in the middle of the sacred design of the Triple Goddess.

Prepare to go deeper. Entering the center of the three rooms, notice that there is a spiral staircase. One step at a time, follow the path lined with burning torches leading counter-clockwise deep into the heart of the Underworld. Hearing a patter of feet you turn to see a gentle wolf that has come to accompany you as a wise guardian and protector.

As you spiral down the path, you begin to breathe more easily and notice that the air is filled with a life-affirming energy. After a while, your surroundings become more luminous, and you realize that a radiant Goddess is now walking with you as well as the wolf. Ask Danu of the tall beautiful people known as the Sidhe if she will accompany you on your journey to Tir Na Ban, The Land of Women. If she agrees, then follow her.

(If not, then simply rest where you are now with the gentle wolf. What is most important is that you become aware of the powerful, nurturing,

and life affirming embrace of the Great Mother. Sometimes we simply need to rest. When you are ready, the wolf will guide you back to surface Earth. There, feel newly refreshed and deeply loved.)

If you decide to travel on with Danu, notice that there is a river in front of you and that a boat is waiting to take you to a distant shore. As you step into the wooden vessel, you notice there is neither a rudder nor oars. Danu stands beside you and the boat sails through the mists, through space, time, and dimension toward Tir Na Ban, the Blessed Isle and Land of Women. Fish leap playfully around the boat as it travels smoothly and swiftly through the water. Suddenly, Danu raises her arms and the mist vanishes. Before you is an emerald green land of blossoming flowers and trees with silver branches that whisper secrets to those who are ready to hear.

Once you feel the boat is against solid ground, step off onto the Blessed Isle. Take a moment to hear the chorus of magical birds. Look down at your feet to see what type of shoes you are wearing, then glance at your clothes. Your garments may be the same, or perhaps they have changed into the colorful attire of the Sidhe.

You follow Danu to a sacred place in the forest where three ancient Beech trees grow. The Mother Goddess closes her eyes, and you realize that she is communing with the trees. Listening closely, you notice that they are also speaking to *you*, offering a message that you need just now. Each sacred grove of three ancient trees opens to a special Otherworld that holds a treasure for you. Like ancient mothers, the Beech trees offer nurturing and caring. For a moment, simply be aware of how you are tended by this natural energy. Perhaps you feel more attuned to nature and the sacred rhythms of your body.

Feeling strong and ready for the next phase of your Quest, you journey on with Danu. As you walk, you notice the vibrant green of the plants and the soothing blues of the water and sky. Soon, you approach a sacred well and begin to walk on a spiral path leading downward toward the source of the water. Danu leans forward and takes a bowl of water from the well, then hands it to you. As you sip the water, you realize it is the sweetest nectar you have ever known. You feel radiantly healthy, whole, and alive. Thank Danu for this great gift of life.

Spend some time gazing at the luminous Otherworld. It is a deeply magical place and you are fortunate to have been invited in to the Land of Women. Know that you can return at any time to sip the nectar of a land that heals.

When you are ready, return to the boat, which you now have the power to steer alone—with the Inner Light of your heart—and then in a clockwise direction travel back up the spiral pathway that leads to the entrance of surface Earth. Know that you are returning to the realm in which humans reside, a place that is currently your sacred home. Remember to thank Danu and her helpers for giving you access to Tir Na Ban. Arrive back into your body, to this point in present time and space—bringing the life-affirming gifts of the Goddess with you.

Danu's Goddess Blessing

I whisper to you

In the space between stars.

My thoughts hold you

Until the time of your awakening

Into the world of form.

Fortunate one,

May you understand

That your life is blessed.

May you open your heart

And receive what life

Is offering you.

CEASAIR

Ceasair in Irish Myth & Legend

Granddaughter of Noah

he early mythology of Ireland is recorded in the medieval Christian work, *The Book of the Taking of Ireland*, (the *Lebor Gabala Erenn)*. It begins with Ceasair, the feisty granddaughter of Noah. She was the daughter of Bith and his wife Birren. There are mystics who claim that the *Lebor Gabala Erenn* is the true early history of Ireland. If it is true, then the Irish are descendants of Noah, therefore the mystical school of Melchizedek. This then means that Ireland and Israel drank from the same well, receiving the transmission of the Tree of Life. In some way Ceasair knew she could speak Ireland into creation. The patron Saints of Ireland, St Brigit and St Patrick, kept the mystical light alive in the heart of Ireland creating a Golden Age. It is possible that a new renaissance of language and culture is burning in the hearts of those with Irish blood even now.

Some poets claim that Ceasair is the embodiment of pagan myth within a biblical story, and it may be that Ceasair replaced the earlier Goddess Banba. Whatever her true origin might be, the myth and legend of Ceasair arises out of our need to defend our lives, our families and what is good and true in this world.

DNA testing is beginning to suggest that the mythological history of Ireland and Britain might be more accurate than scientists have previously believed. The legend of Ceasair, whether fact or fiction, presents us with a woman strong enough to defy the patriarchy, building her own ark and setting sail with her friends and family to a new land. It is likely that Ceasair's story was written to replace the legend of the Goddess Banba and her two sisters, Fodhla and Eriu, the original triple Goddesses of Ireland. If we listen carefully, we may discover an even more ancient voice whispering between the worlds.

Ceasair's story is one of a woman brave enough to live into the Divine Feminine. The *Lebor Gabala Erenn* states that Ceasair and her group of fifty women and three men sailed from Egypt through raging storms to eventually reach Spain. Then, for nine days, they continued on, until landing at the coast of Ireland in *Dún na mBarc*, now known as Bantry Bay in County Cork.

Ceasair's landing in Ireland is dated 3200 BC. As I sense into her story, I feel my ancestral roots pulling toward the Emerald Isle. In this moment, Ceasair lives within and around me. This is the story as she sends it from the past into the present, through dreams and visions. Now we will travel back in time more than five thousand years to catch a glimpse of an empowered female ancestor who embodies willpower and steadfastness. In legends, she perishes in a flood. However, in the tradition of the Goddess, it is more likely that she walked between the worlds to Tir Na Ban.

Ceasair Speaks
Ireland's Missing Tale

As I gaze towards the north, I see green grass and rain-soaked trees sparkling like polished emeralds. Behind me is a cold, grey sea from which we have emerged with our lives. Ladra, our pilot, has laid a circle of seventy-two stones in the damp earth and is preparing a fire with smoldering branches. We gather around, awaiting the warmth of this new hearth. Fifty women and three men stand in circles thanking the Goddess Eriu and her sisters, Banba and Fodhla, for leading us through storms, currents, and waves to this sacred island.

My name is Ceasair. I am the daughter of Bith and granddaughter of Noah. Now a woman by right, my destiny began when my grandfather built an ark of gopherwood. He gathered our family together and told us that a storm was coming and that humanity might not survive. He also explained that only his wife, six children, and a variety of animals would be allowed to board the ark. Even as his granddaughter, I was not amongst the chosen few. I saw how the light flashed when he walked, and I spoke to him as invisible forces blew his hair and clothes. I did not doubt that a flood was coming, but I did not understand why God would not include me as among the chosen.

I asked what I had done to be rejected. Noah said that those of the lineage of Cain—who had killed his brother, Abel—would not be allowed to live. I was confused by the idea that Cain, a man I had never met, might in some ways still defiantly live in my blood and be the cause of my demise. At night, I whispered to Cain, who seemed to reside in the shadows of caves and dark places. I asked God and the Goddess to forgive my ancestors, to release me from my bondage, and to set me on a new course in which I might live and my children thrive. My grandfather, Noah, had to follow his destiny—and I had to follow mine.

Dreams and visions from the Great Mother visited, telling me that I must build a ship for myself and my loved ones, and that our course had already been set. Like my grandfather, I spoke about the storms that would arrive—but most people laughed.

The visions that came to me at night showed an emerald island that seemed far away, across a cold, grey sea. The Earth herself spoke to me, as a mother would call her child. The sensations that resonated from deep within her soil were insistent. I knew that the dream of my life was intertwined with the stones, leaves and branches of that land in a way I could not explain. Even though I stood far away, my feet already knew the hills and valleys of the new, green earth. Egypt was spitting me out, along with my sisters and some men. Why, Goddess, are we so unloved?

I did not have the carpentry skills that Grandfather possessed, but I had learned to use my knife and ax, as well as ropes. I had been taught to sew, cook, and even weave magic; and so I gathered the materials required to weave a dream together. As I collected what we would need for our voyage, I sensed that, if I listened carefully, no one would go hungry within the walls of my ship. When I prayed, I knew what to gather. Like my grandfather, I was also guided. Those of the spirit world walked with me.

I could see Noah pacing with his long hair now a tousled, wild mess and his crazed eyes looking for the first sign of a storm. I wondered if my dark hair was as tangled as his. In a way, I did not mind his rejection, because he had set me free to live into my own destiny.

I harvested herbs for every ill, roots for soups, and sweet grasses for the horses that would accompany us. I built my ship on the edge of town where few noticed that I was doing the work of both men and women. I was building out the hull of an unused sea vessel that I had found, and I wove a roof to keep the rain out.

It was at this point that I discovered my body had become lighter. I could jump and glide onto the main deck and walk on the bowsprit. The pole for the stays should have broken, but somehow, it remained balanced and weightless. I felt as though a force that I could trust was beginning to work through me.

Over time, some people came to assist in the creation of my ship. Fintan, the poet and seer, and eventually my father, Bith, and my brother, Ladra, joined in, as well as other friends and family members that Noah had turned away. Ladra had been trained as a pilot. He brought a rudder that he installed, and oars, and offered his knowledge of the stars. I told him that there would be no stars, but only the darkest of nights for a very long time. He looked at me blankly for a moment and said that he was trained for storms. He did not fully understand, and I did not wish to frighten him. I knew the Goddess would guide us safely to our new home.

The night the clouds began to gather, I heard the Great Mother whisper that I must leave immediately and go with my family, friends, and horses to the ship. I had found a conch shell and had prepared it to be a signal of the departure time, and I blew into it with all my stregth.

Soon, fifty women and three men walked aboard the ship, along with my stallion and three mares. Thunder shook the boat and lightning flashed, and, for a moment, I saw Noah's ark shake as if wishing to free itself. Then suddenly, the water rose up, tsunamis came in from all directions, and the skies went dark. Now on board, we all held onto one another as the water took hold of the ship and tossed it like a child's plaything. Our makeshift boat survived because the Goddess held it like a beloved work of art. She had a plan for us, a destiny that we would fulfill as time passed. It was thrilling, even though it was dark, and horses and people were thrashed about.

I have no idea how long the tempest lasted, but eventually, a great stillness prevailed. For a few days, the ship sat quietly in darkness, as if waiting for a pulse from the Great Mother. I could hear people crying, but I listened intently for the commands I knew would come. I did not fear our situation, but trusted in an even greater Light. There was no way to know where we were, or how long we would be at sea. All I knew was that the Emerald Isles were calling and that eventually, I would find home.

"Go outside now!" I finally heard the Goddess say. I obeyed immediately and went out onto the bow of the ship. Once again I felt weightless. "Find the Light within your heart and throw it to me. I will guide you," said the voice.

I wondered briefly what the Goddess meant. Then I felt a Light shining from my heart, bright enough to light up the bow of the ship. I grasped the Light in my hands, and I threw and breathed and imagined it out across the cold, black sea, as far as I could. The ship lurched forward, and without rudder or oars, our destiny was set in motion.

I did not move from the bow, focusing on the path that stretched before us. The voice called to me, singing as a mother sings to her child. I knew as I continued to send the Light of my heart out before us into the sea that my ancestors had been forgiven for any errors. I willed the ship through the velvety black, salty silence and across the seemingly endless sea to a promised land.

Visions came to me of the children I would have with Fintan, and the children other women would also have with him. I could see their hair shifting over generations from dark to red, and brown skins turning pale. I envisioned a strong race of human beings living for centuries amongst green grasses, cold, flowing streams, and grey stones. I heard the songs of the bards and the lines of the poets, and I smelled the herbs gathered by wise women. For the first time, I was certain I was going to my true home.

As I gazed ahead, I could see what seemed to be a portal opening up. It was pulling me, sucking me into it. The Light became so bright that I nearly fainted, but I willed myself to stand, clinging tightly to the wood that was fastened on the front of the ship. Shades circled me, calling me names and challenging me to jump into the deep water while I still had a chance. I ignored them. Creatures with manes of seaweed and heads like horses rose up from the sea and said that Cain was calling me to the Underworld. Again, I ignored these ghosts.

The Light then became like a brightly burning fire. The cold from the voyage that had clung to me burned off and I was flying in the Light. I could perceive winged beings like angels all around me, and they were singing. I hummed with them, although my voice could not match their celestial tones. It seemed as though we were moving fast, but at the same time, hardly moving at all. And then the Light went out.

My body slid to the floor of the ship's bow just as Fintan came out from below deck.

"Do not die, my beloved," he pleaded. "We are nearly there."

"I cannot die," I said weakly. "We have six children coming. I have seen their smiling faces. I need my herbs."

Fintan left me and returned soon with a strong brew made with the herbs I'd gathered to sustain us all during the passage. It brought life back into my cold body.

"Come inside," he urged me.

"I cannot, because the Goddess is anchored to my heart, and she is pulling us home," I told him.

He tried to carry me, but I was stuck fast to the bow of the ship. Eventually, Fintan simply stood beside me and called out, "Goddess, please also use my body and heart to bring us to you!"

All night long, we stayed together and the Goddess used us. It was an interesting lovemaking, for only our hips touched. I could feel his body beside me, and I believe our bodies touching created enough warmth so that we lived through the night. He received the current, and I pulled the strands of moonbeams through my body, with stars whirling past, as we raced to our new land.

In the morning, I opened my eyes to sunlight flashing upon the dark sea. Then I gazed up to see Fintan standing and staring out across the horizon.

"Look!" Fintan cried out. "Look!"

Some people ran to port and others ran starboard, but we were all straining to see the island off in the distance. My stallion began to paw and neigh, thrashing his white mane and baring his teeth at the mares. People scattered as he rounded up his herd and moved toward the gangplank door, which had lost a hinge but was still tied shut with rope.

A luminous being was walking on the water toward us. She seemed so familiar that my heart was filled with joy. Soon, she was standing in the water in front of the ship. The Goddess must have been at least thirteen feet tall, with long, red hair that flowed down past her knees. Her body was radiant with health and life, and her face was the most attractive I have ever seen.

The Goddess spoke with great authority and wisdom: "I am Eriu, Goddess of this abundant land. I have called you to be here and live with me. All that I ask is that you love me and one another, that you raise and share food with each other, and that you always live in peace. As long as you do these things, this land will flourish. But if you quarrel, this land will also despair."

I bowed my head toward her, honoring her request. I said, "I understand, and so do my people." As I uttered those words, I wished fervently that it would always be true.

Eriu gazed deeply into my eyes for a few moments, as if looking through me into the future. "The future is not yet decided," she said at last. When she spoke, I felt a rush of heat run down my spine.

Eriu nodded, indicating that we should follow, then turned and led our ship past rocks and islands to a bay where the waters were calm. Once there, she gently pulled us to land. We lowered the gangplank to let the horses out first. The stallion breathed in deeply, and then, snorting, stepped carefully down the plank, wondering if he could trust the wood. He made a final leap onto land and neighed, curious if there were other horses close by. No whinny was heard in response. His mares then followed him, jumping and leaping when they reached the damp soil. They nosed the tall grasses and began to graze.

Slowly, my family and friends stumbled out of the ship and onto land. They held on to one another, crying, singing, laughing, and dancing. "Eriu," they cried out, "we love you!"

I share this story for my sons and daughters, my grandchildren, and the generations of children beyond them. I speak to you, all my children, because I want you to remember me and know that I am sending you gifts through thousands of years to help you end your darkness and claim the Light that is already yours. Know that, in any moment, you can choose to release yourself from ancestries of pain and suffering and choose a new life for yourself. You can live as your own wild and unique self. I am still a co-walker.

We come from the Light and our True Nature is that of strength, creativity, fertility, abundance, and happiness. We are separate and yet inherently a part of all that is. We are each an unforgettable fragment of a web of life that is eternal. Let us remember Eriu and love her, love one another, and live in peace.

Looking into the future, I can see that there will be those who will say that Ceasair perished in the flood and that only the poet Fintan survived. The truth is that Fintan's words survived because he was a poet, and eventually his words were written down. My story was changed to match the demands of the time. I tell you today that I lived and I live on now. Those of you who tap into me now will also live on.

Healing with Ceasair

Finding Ceasair
Saint Patrick & The Serpents

Ceasair is associated with Banba, one of the original triple Goddesses of Ireland. Her celebration day is shared each year with Saint Patrick around March 17, when many people celebrate the cultural history of Ireland. In Celtic legend, it is said that Saint Patrick battled a large serpent and, after slaying it, the waters of the lake (which became known as Lough Derg) turned red, thus gaining its name. However, there were no snakes in Ireland after the Ice Age. Perhaps St Patrick did banish distorted spirits, which are sometimes compared to slithering serpents as they attempt to deviate from their elevation. In other words, St Patrick had the gift of anchoring the supernal light.

St Patrick also rid Ireland of the old religious practices of the Druids, and in doing so a great deal of the wisdom of the Celts was either absorbed into Christianity or lost. Perhaps one day we will evolve enough to end the domination, violence and control, and instead learn from the rituals and practices of earlier people and differing religions. Some say that when the Messiah returns in the guise of Moses, Jesus, Arthur, Buddha (perhaps in the form of a woman) or perhaps within our selves, the wolves and lions will lay down with the sheep. This implies that in the process of the integration of our body, mind and spirit, we will have elevated to higher levels of wisdom, acceptance and understanding.

Serpents are intimately connected with Goddess worship, and they are often depicted twining around her staff. The oldest known image of two snakes coiling up a staff was found in an area of modern-day southern Iraq, known then as Sumer, and dates to 2000 BC. The serpent deities are ancient symbols of creative life force, fertility, healing, and immortality.

Avebury in South West England is said to be the site of an earth serpent. Norse mythology describes Jormungand, the serpent that encircles the world, representing both creation and destruction. In many indigenous cultures, snakes are honored for their ability to shed their skin and renew themselves. The ancient Chinese connected the snake with rain, which brings life to the Earth. Hindu myths also contain many tales of serpents, including the snake Goddess Kadru who gave birth to a thousand children; one of them was Shesha, whom the Gods used to churn many things into being—including the moon.

With the Christianization of Ireland, the Celts and the early monks shared creative but conflicting beliefs. Due to a literal interpretation of the story of Adam and Eve, the serpent became associated with women, destruction, jealousy and the fall of humankind from the state of perfection. In some versions of the story the snake is Lilith, an original Mother Goddesses and the first wife of Adam. In Judaism there are two trees in the Garden of Eden, the Tree of Life and the Tree of Knowledge. It was Lilith who suggested that Eve taste the forbidden fruit. Perhaps for that reason Lilith is said to sit at the base of the Tree of Knowledge, or the Tree of Evil, tempting humankind. It is Lilith that is said to have released concealed evil inserted into an apple or fig, allowing it to spread. Until the 1960s, Lilith was thought of as the ultimate demon that distracted humankind from its true purpose, and her role of Mother Goddess was forgotten. Is it possible that Lilith is responsible for gnosis, or Self-knowing? Lilith's archetype has been used by the feminist movement as inspiration for freedom seeking, independent women. Perhaps like many of the Goddesses in these pages, Lilith is being re-examined and understood. Today Lilith is a female symbol of sexual control, sovereignty and free will.

If we switch from religious parables and interpretations for a moment and switch to a psychological understanding of archetypes, we can see that each of these figures can be found as aspects of our own psyche. Ultimately all of the archetypes that live and act within us need to be elevated through knowledge, comprehension and wisdom. We must keep in mind that spiritual stories are meant to convey wisdom and are not meant to be taken literally. There is nothing wrong with snakes and women are not inherently evil! When we heal and embrace our shadows, we can reclaim our essential power. Stories teach us that there is a difference between the forces of life, and the forces of confusion and destruction.

The Cosmic Mother force, known as the Shekinah (or in esoteric Christianity as Sophia), can lead us back to the Tree of Life, in other words, the wholeness of our body, mind and spirit. The dance of the divine mother and father can never be separated, for they are part of the dance of totality.

Misunderstanding the symbolism of the snake, Saint Patrick (c. AD 385–461) sought to put an end to the practice of the Druids and Goddess worship, and the snake (no longer seen as the wise and life-supportive element of the Earth) became a sign of evil. However, Saint Patrick brought an incredible amount of light to Ireland. The early Druids practiced oral storytelling, and the traditions of the Celts could have been destroyed and lost, like the mythology of the Picts, who lived in what is now eastern and northern Ireland and Scotland. Luckily, Saint Patrick founded monastery schools and churches. Because of his industriousness, early Irish histories and stories were written down. During the 6th and 7th centuries (while the rest of Europe floundered in the Dark Ages), Irish monastic schools flourished as centers of learning and scholarship. We need to look back and thank Saint Patrick for protecting illuminated Christian manuscripts and also for preserving Celtic myths and legends.

March 17 is a day to remember that green is the color of compassion and of the heart. It's a good day to forgive our own blind spots and ignorance as well as the errors of those who came before us. It is a day to honor the wisdom that has been handed down through many cultures and to bless nature, particularly the life-affirming serpent. As the age of domination ends, it becomes likely that the Triple Goddess and the Saint are recognizing each other's wisdom and are learning to appreciate each other in the Otherworlds. We can support their union by coming to peace with the archetypal forces that live within us.

Ceasair in Nature
Alder, Horse & Hawk

Ceasair has a fondness for Alder trees, perhaps because they are the first to grow after a fire or devastation. They were used in old Europe to build boats, oars, and bridges. You can recognize Alders by their fruit (inch-long cones called *strobili*) that contain seeds that birds and small animals use as winter food. To the Druids, the Alder is a tree of protection. The flowers are used as charms in Faery magic, and they are helpful as a flower essence, when the going gets tough.

In the lineage of Noah and his Ark, many reptiles, birds, and animals are under Ceasair's protection. The Serpent or Dragon is an ancient symbol of Banba and potentially Ceasair as well, who would have known something of the healing arts. In world mythology, Goddesses often appear as Dragons.

Ceasair arrived on the shores of Ireland with her herd of horses, symbolic of power and the ability to stay in touch with the realm of Spirit. Ceasair's sacred bird is the Hawk, symbolizing wisdom, intuition, and truth. The Hawk has broad vision and the ability to move gracefully between parallel dimensions.

Ceasair's Colors
Deep Red, White, & Olive

Ceasair's three sacred colors are Deep Red, White, and Olive. Each color is symbolic of a quality or gift that the Goddess possesses. Deep Ruby Red is the color of strength and survival. It is used as an essence when planting seeds within Earth or to encourage the roots of plants to grow. Red invites us to rise up straight and strong like a tree. Ceasair encourages an entire tribe to flourish. Deep Red is connected to fire, the dreams of Earth and the life that wishes to emerge like sparks remembering their wholeness.

White is a combination of all the colors and is linked to the soul qualities of willpower and of steadfastness. When the essence of White opens within us, it can feel as though a mountain is supporting us and we have what it takes to endure. White Light can lead, guide, direct, and protect us with precision and accuracy, even (like Ceasair) through the stormiest night.

Olive is the color of feminine empowerment. It supports us in a grounded, yet spacious, way as we go on adventures to discover more about the truth of who we are. It is the color of new beginnings, symbolized by the dove and the olive branch of hope. This combination is called "Ancestral Spirit."

Meeting the Goddess Ceasair

The Triple Goddesses of Ireland—Eriu, Fodhla and Banba—are ancient, wise beings who have been tending the landscape for centuries. If you call upon the Goddesses, they may accompany you as co-walkers or guides of Light and Wisdom to help you on your hero's or heroine's journey. The easiest way to access them is to walk amongst sacred sites in Ireland. If you cannot travel that far, simply place your hand on the illustrations in this book and allow your spirit to take you there. We are never more than a thought away from one another.

The Goddess Ceasair knew how to access her Inner Light, which was necessary in order to achieve her Quest. The Goddess Eriu recognized this and helped bring Ceasair to shore so she could plant the seeds of the Goddess traditions of Ireland. The soul qualities that Ceasair helps us remember are discipline, willpower and faith.

Practice
Building a Place of Personal Refuge

When it is time for us to take a Quest or face something that challenges us, the only way through the storm is to face it directly. It is the time when we need to stay focused on the positive, and as much as possible resist the tendency to be broken by negativity. The purpose of the ark is to protect and preserve the lives and beliefs of the people that are dear to us. In Latin the word "*arcēre*" means to hold off or defend against. It is important to have a sanctuary where we can feel at peace, restore and renew. The archetypal structure of the ark also exists inside our souls. Within each of us is a sacred treasure or Grail, our eternal light that can never be destroyed. Our positive words and actions can carry us through the darkest of times.

Today observe your thoughts. Notice how often you use negative words, and how often you use positive words.

Refrain from speaking against yourself or another. Focus instead on the light that exists within everyone and everything. The more we can discipline ourselves and work with positive words, sounds and energies, the more quickly we can build a place of personal refuge within and around ourselves.

Visualization
Three Stars & A Dragon

Imagine that you are in the middle of the Celtic sea. The swirling, cosmic waters are full of potential, and also dragons. Take a deep breath and feel into where you are on your current life journey. Know that if you stay connected to your Inner Light, you can overcome all challenges.

Peer into the night sky and locate the three stars of Orion's Belt. These stars are a reminder that we all have three stars within our light bodies designed to lead, guide, direct, and protect us.

Dragons are a symbol of the Great Goddess. As you align with your starry origin, the dragons may decide to carry you on their backs. This means your life will be blessed with creativity, health, and success. Let's locate the three stars now.

To locate your first inner star, measure two finger widths below your navel and imagine traveling two finger widths inside. In your energy belly, you can locate a shining star. Close your eyes and see if you can feel the gentle pulse of this star that loves your body and your life. This is your **Incarnational Star,** the first light that came into your body during your conception. This first spark of your unique life contains the colors and sounds that are sacred to you. The Incarnational Star is the part of you that is eternal and will never die. Listen gently and see if you can become increasingly aware of the colors and sounds of your unique star. This is very healthy for your body.

Raise your awareness to your chest. The second star, the **Heart Star,** resides energetically in the center of your chest, the area associated with the emerald green quality of compassion. This is the inner place where you can get to know your Soul. When you enter this dimension of your consciousness, you can tap into the world of dreams and imagination. You can soar freely on Ceasair's Winged Horse through the universe and find magical portals and dimensions to explore. Calling on the purity of your emerald light, you unbind yourself from karma and align with your ancient, angelic nature. The Heart Star is a place of freedom, love, and compassion, qualities that are always available to you.

The third star is known as your **Crown of Light Star.** It tends to open as a pulsation of light in your forehead and then expand upwards as a light or halo over your head. As you become aware of this shining star or pulsing light, your connection to the wise, ancient ones becomes stronger and more accessible. This radiant star is aligned with your personal brilliancy. This is not the intelligence of the ego, but something much vaster and infinitely more creative. Your Higher Self is aligned with the all-encompassing intelligence of the universe that loves everything beyond belief.

When all three stars align, you may feel a Circle of Light open and surround your entire body. This is the Infinite Light that will be your best friend during your Grail Quest.

On your journey, remember to stay aligned with your three stars. From this place of attunement, you will never lose your way. Remain in your body, aware and present in every situation. We do not need to fully understand our life purpose and mission, or even why we feel we need to find the Grail. Our soul already knows the destiny we need to live into on this journey. All we need to do is throw the Light of our hearts into the future and trust in the process of life. You may feel a Dragon coming to carry you to a greater destiny even now.

Ceasair's Light Blessing

Each morning a flower blossoms just for you.

Go outside and see if you can feel its message.

Walk in nature and learn her language.

May you be blessed with ears that hear the colors

Of the moon, wind and stars, for their melody is all

Around you if you look with the eyes of your heart.

There are thin places on Earth

Where wise ones design symbols for our souls

So that we never forget our origins.

May your heart be strong and filled

With ample light to cross any ocean

Or walk through any illusion that binds you.

May wisdom surround and protect you

Through every day and night of your life.

May you learn the colors and melodies of your soul.

May you find the spark of this blessing

And trust that love and goodness

Will always carry you Home.

AINE

Aine in Myth & Legend

A Solar Goddess

A ine's name means "brightness" or "splendor," and her qualities include joy, brilliance, creativity, and fame. An independent Goddess, Aine prefers shining her own Light. She is a six-foot-tall, green-eyed Goddess and one that you want to have as an ally, for like the sun, she possesses a radiant and life-affirming, protective Light. Aine helps all that she loves stay aligned with goodness and illumination. In Irish mythology, it is said that Aine can lift twenty-five tons and either rides on or shape-shifts into the fastest red mare on Earth, a horse by the name of Lair Derg. Aine's love is so deep and true that she burns away what is false within each of us so we can find our own Light. Her Light is still luminous during the nighttime hours, and for this reason, she can be mistaken for a lunar Goddess. The most powerful Faery in Ulster was Aynia, who may have been another guise of Aine. With such a big heart, she does not mind what time of the day or night you call to her, or what season of the year, although she is generally associated with daylight, fire, and the warmer months.

Solar Goddesses do not exist in Greek or Roman mythology. We need to travel back in time to find Goddesses of the sun. Aine or Enya is an invulnerable Irish Goddess, a member of the Tuatha Dé Danann, a group of enlightened beings who assisted in the terra-forming of the land of Ireland and Britain. For thousands of years, they walked on Earth in luminous light bodies until they retreated to the Otherworlds.

For those who wish to connect with Aine as an ally, there are several areas of the Irish landscape where you may still commune with her. The most prominent is Aine's hill and meadow, located in County Limerick, Ireland. Rites in her honor were practiced there, and *Cnoc Aine* (Aine's hill, but officially, in English, the hill of Knockainey near Lough Gur) is acknowledged as Aine's power spot. The rounded hill has three rings or barrows where some say she pours her energy, giving warmth and life to the Earth. She is a fertile Goddess, and those she smiles upon prosper.

However, you do not have to travel to Ireland, for there are many ways to know Aine. It is possible to sit in the sunlight and connect to her through meditation by just repeating her name until her warmth comes into you. You can also sun gaze with closed eyes and draw the last of the evening rays into your body, allowing their radiance to fill you with her life force.

The most prominent myths of Aine associate her with the Mother Goddess, Danu. Aine's lovers included both Gods and mortals. In some myths, Aine became the wife of King Ailill, but that is the tale of people who misunderstood the Goddess of Sovereignty. Because they prefer shining their own light to reflecting the light of another, Solar Goddesses seldom make good wives. Aine honored her independence and freedom above all men. In legend, the Goddess Aine eventually becomes the lover of the Sea God, Manannan Mac Lir. Some scholars say that Aine's descendants are those of the Geraldines and the Fitzgeralds. Her sister is the Goddess, Grian (pronounced "green"), who might be a form Aine takes during the winter months.

Aine was absorbed into Celtic Christianity as Saint Anne, and she was celebrated until the 19th century. Her special feast was held on Midsummer Eve (Summer Solstice), when a fire was lit in her honor and the land was blessed. Sometimes referred to as Aine Chlair, Aine has the reputation of being the best-hearted woman who ever existed. Even now, it is said that she still comes to those in need.

Aine Speaks
Ireland's Missing Tale

I am like a white diamond journeying through space. There are stars as far as I can see and feel. I breathe in the vast expanse and breathe out Light. My name is Aine. I have been sent from an ancient past to weave sunbeams into messages for you. For a long time, I was forgotten, except by children who played with sparkling stones at the edges of brooks and flowing streams. Even the water needs the sunlight now. As the thirst increases on the Earth for what is good, true, and real, I am called to return to you and share my story.

"Hurry up, there are those who need you," my mother said. Although her voice sounded insistent, I noticed that she moved slowly, like the wind blowing gently through a field of tall grasses. It was dawn, and she was planting seeds along the southern edge of a meadow that stretched out between her sacred Beech trees and the ancient Oaks. A spring fed the multi-colored flowers that were in bloom around her.

Mother took my hand and led me over to the eastern side of the meadow, where blue and purple morning glories were beginning to open. "Shine your Light here," she said, as the emerging daylight began prompting the flowers to unfurl and open.

"How?" I asked. "How do I give my Light to these flowers to help them grow?"

"The same way you help all creation grow. Close your eyes, focus on your heart, entwine your Light with the rays of the sun, and fill all creation with your love."

I was but a child when I learned to align with creation. I loved the way I felt standing next to my mother, who seemed so ancient, so wise, and so beautiful, all at the same time. I noticed, as I poured my love into the morning glories, that they did indeed respond, and soon their flowers were wide open.

"Now go to the honeysuckle and practice with him," said my mother.

The honeysuckle vine was soon covered in large, golden flowers, and in a little while, his irresistible scent was wafting across the meadow, attracting bees and butterflies.

"Come here," my mother said sharply. The tone of her voice was enough to let me know it was time to hide. We both stepped into the forest and I scrambled up into the branches of a large oak.

I could see something moving through the meadow. At first, it seemed like smoke, because the energy was so dense. After a while, my vision cleared and I realized that it was a boy who was weeping. He was holding a dead squirrel he had shot with his bow and arrows. I wanted to go closer to him, but just my thought of this made him spin around quickly. The boy then drew an arrow into his bow and pulled it back taut. He did not see me, but I noticed that the squirrel was now hanging limply across his shoulder. The boy turned and ran north into the thick of the forest.

Mother and I went to see the family of young squirrels who now had to live without their own mother.

"Will they live?" I asked her.

"Some of them," she told me, placing nuts and seeds at the entrance of the hollow of the dead tree where they dwelled. "The strong ones will live for a while."

"But Mother," I protested, "we must help them live!"

I started to cry and my mother turned toward me, sending me her warmth.

"Weeping for those who die or struggle will not help them," she said with kindness in her voice. "Instead, if you want to help all living things, then help them stay connected to their Inner Light."

"That Light is eternal," I said, now understanding the wisdom behind her words.

"That boy is training to be a hunter, even though he does not wish to be one." My mother put her warm hand on my shoulder and looked lovingly into my eyes. "He must eat to survive, so we must not judge him."

"Then why did we hide from him, Mother?" I asked. "Why didn't we show him how to work with life and not against it?"

"There are times for all things," she said. "When he is older, he will return to the west side of this meadow, sit by the threshold of the flowing spring, and ask to remember the ways of the Goddess. At that time, we can share with him—but not before."

"But Mother," I repeated, this time stomping my feet on the ground, "why did we hide?"

"Because our Light is so bright that it could harm those who are not ready to know us."

"We could ... could ... hurt people?" I stammered. "But we love and support all life!"

"When the sun shines in the middle of the afternoon, you cannot look upon it with human eyes," she told me. "Only at dawn and dusk, when just a portion of the sun is present in the sky, can people gaze upon her life-affirming rays. All Sun Goddesses are like this too; they can only be seen at dawn and dusk, when the time is right for the human observer."

Mother went back out to the meadow, and she continued to help the leaves and flowers unfurl and the butterflies burst from their cocoons. When she was in the field, the plants did not need the seasons to bring them to full blossom. Her presence was enough. Everywhere she walked, life flourished. Even the flowing streams increased the sound of their music when Danu was close. I tried walking in her footsteps, but the Light from my hands seemed to make plants wither. Danu turned to observe me and laughed. Feeling the wish to go in a new direction, I drew back my hands.

"Could I become a human?" I asked.

"You are a Goddess, but you may take a denser human form if you wish."

"I would like to become a red mare," I said, pretending to gallop around the meadow.

"Perhaps when you are older," said my mother.

Suddenly it was clear to me what I truly wanted. The feelings sprang up within my body with such vigor that they surprised me. "I wish to go to that boy and teach him the ways of love," I told her.

My mother looked at me, then above and behind me. "I can see that you love him and your destiny is intertwined with his," she said. "He is one of the Fitzgerald clan."

I felt a thrill rise up in my heart and I sensed that a great adventure was coming.

"You may go to him," she said. From the tone in Mother's voice, I thought for a moment that she almost seemed sad. "But you will live for thousands of years and his lifespan is brief. When your time with him is done, you must return to me."

I turned north and began to walk toward my destiny.

"Just remember, he will only see part of you," she called out. I smiled and waved to her.

As I stepped into the thick forest, she added, "If you ever find yourself in any trouble or danger, throw the Light of your heart out to me. I will come to you. I am never farther away than the shining sun, or the moon that reflects her light."

"I am the sun that never fails," I said to her. "I will return."

Eager to embrace my new life, I strode quickly along the paths made by deer. As I walked, I grew smaller. My body became increasingly dense and my hair grew darker. I marveled at these changes. I could feel brambles tearing at my ankles and rough stones under my bare feet.

When the boy was only a short distance away, I made a bird sound from the path in the woods. He turned and looked at me but did not raise his bow. He blinked a few times at me, as if adjusting to the light.

"Who are you?" he asked with wonder in his voice.

"I am Aine," I replied.

The boy's name was Codal. After meeting me in the forest, he took me into his kingdom. With my assistance, he became a respected Danann *taoiseach* to his people—a chieftain and light-bearer. We loved each other very much, and after several years, we had three daughters.

Everyone knew that there was something different about me. It was not just that I was a head taller than the other women and most of the men; I also held a unique radiance and did not age rapidly like those around me.

It did not take me long to realize that women were primarily thought of as housekeepers and child-bearers in Codal's community. I was not troubled, since I wished to experience motherhood and discover what it was to be loved and to live with my beloved. Although I could lift a boulder with little effort, I allowed the men in the kingdom to tend to me. It was a very peaceful and happy period of my life.

As I explored the world of men and women, I had only the greatest regard for all creatures upon the Earth. Before this, nothing that was challenging or difficult had ever been part of my world. Certainly, there had been flowers that wilted, and I had seen animals cross beyond this world. But in my new life, I discovered that the human world was wrought with many challenges.

Still, I knew that I would return to the forest to be with Mother Danu after some number of years had passed. I believe Codal knew that about me, also. Sometimes, when I rode my red mare in the rain and fog, my beloved would call out to me as though he was afraid he might lose me. I did still have the ability to slip between the veils of life and death, but I was fascinated by my husband and by the experience of my changing form as my babies grew within me.

There would be periods when my beloved Codal would be called off to battle. I felt somewhat estranged in our earthen fortress, and I missed him. He never knew how many men I threw over the grey stone walls of our kingdom, or how much I enjoyed my strength. In fact, I protected all the children in our kingdom.

One night, I was awakened by the sounds of screaming and the smell of fire. I looked out my window and could see that there were strange men in the courtyard. I did not feel frightened, for I knew I would not die, yet I did sense that something momentous was about to occur.

The door to my bedroom was forced open and I saw Ailill Olom, the King of Ireland, standing there. I thought he was quite handsome. He was young, strong, and muscular. He pointed his sword in my direction, looking at me with eyes that seemed to have been made of coals knocked from the cook's feasting fire. I knew the King desired me, but he was not my beloved, so I turned away from him. He seemed outraged by my movement, for suddenly he was upon me—and his dark hair mingled with mine.

But the Goddess only entertains men when she is ready, and so I bit his ear and did not release it until he released me. He screamed and raged at me while blood poured into my lips, but I still did not release it. His men came and beat me, trying to remove me from their king. Even so, he was not liberated until he finally pulled back hard. When Ailill did, he realized his ear was left in my teeth.

That was the moment to throw my Light to my mother, Danu. She must have heard me already, because she was there so quickly. Danu stood between me and the now-disfigured King Ailill Olom.

Danu rose to her greatest height and, towering above the man, she said, "You are maimed and now disqualified to be a king. May you learn from your errors."

Ailill Olom backed out of the room with his men; then, they turned and fled.

Danu watched from a window as they climbed upon horses and made a hasty retreat. Then she turned to me and said, "It is time for you to return to me."

She took the King's ear and folded it inside her skirts. She wiped my face, and the tenderness of her touch brought tears to my eyes.

"You remain unharmed," said Danu. "Anything that happens to you in this world will never touch your Light. You carry a child which Ailill will claim as his, but the child is of the Goddess."

"Thank you, Mother," I murmured.

As she spoke to me, I felt her cleansing waves. Simply uttering her name—Danu, Danu, Danu—cleansed every part of my being. And then I felt the sun within me. It glowed, radiated, and burned away all fear and pain.

"Will the King live?" I asked Danu.

"If you allow him to live," she answered. "And if you do, he will be more honorable for his loss." She looked in front of me, behind me, and then into my eyes and added, "But you must come home now."

"If I refuse to be his wife, I know that they will hunt me," I replied sadly.

"The time of the Sun Goddess is over on Earth for quite a while," said Danu. "One day, people will learn that there is no way to destroy what is beautiful and good."

"What will become of Codal?" I asked my mother.

She looked off into the distance as if reading time and space, and then said: "The *taoiseach* will follow you in his own time to the meadow where he found you. He will bring the children there and, facing west, he will learn the ways of the Goddess."

I smiled brightly, thinking about all of us in the meadow together.

"But he will cross from there into the next world," she added, taking my hand and placing it on her large breasts. I could feel the pulsing of her heart. As her words registered, I also knew that a cycle must run its course, and so I nodded.

We did not take horses but walked through portals, slipping between worlds so we could not be traced. It was wonderful to feel my light body again as we moved quickly and without effort through dimensions. When I time travel, I always head directly to my sacred tree, the oak, because it has a cosmic wisdom that welcomes me home. When we stepped out of the heart of the great oak and into the meadow, I went out to greet each plant, tree, and flower. You know when you have been away for a while because the landscape changes. Yet the earth was the same, and my feet luxuriated in the loamy soil, sweet green grasses, and yellow flowers.

It was several years before my husband returned to our field. In the meantime, I watched my children grow through sky-glasses, which we can peer into when we love someone greatly. Although I could not raise them, I could see that they were growing into the demi-gods they were meant to be. The children felt my presence. At times, when they were in danger or were thinking about some mischievous action, they would turn and look toward the sun or the bright side of the moon. Then they chose what was brightest or best.

Toward the end of his life, Codal began to feel drawn back to the meadow. Goddesses do not age, and so I looked the same as I stepped from the Otherside to meet him. His hair was entirely grey, but his eyes were the same. When he saw me, he smiled and reached for my hands.

"You were my beloved from the time I first saw you," he said. A tear trickled down his cheek. He took a deep breath, as if filling up with all things that are good, and then said, "Thank you, my darling Aine. You are the best-hearted woman that ever lived. My life with you has been good."

We sat in the meadow together enjoying the scent of the yellow blossoms. But soon, his breath shortened and he put his head in my lap. I sang to him and stroked his hair as his spirit began to depart to an Otherworld reserved for heroes. For a few moments, he crossed back and forth on the Rainbow Bridge.

"I will find you again in another life," I said as his breath grew faint. "And next time, let us not be torn away from each other by war but ..."

He finished my sentence for me: "... may we be united in love and peace."

And with that, the rays of the sun engulfed him in their warmth and carried him, ever so gently, to his next kingdom. He did not look back at me. Perhaps he was amazed by the show of Lights that the Devas and Goddesses gave him to celebrate his life.

It has been 5,125 years and I am still here. My beloved Codal has yet to meet me in my world. The Sea God, Manannan Mac Lir, wooed me, and we spent a delightful three-hundred-year honeymoon under the seas. Eventually, he began to love another. Each of us has our own time with someone.

One day, I left Mac Lir's watery bed and returned to Danu's meadow. When she saw me, my mother simply smiled and continued singing to the blue and violet morning glories. I loved hearing the songs as they echoed along the rivers and through the forest.

I know that, one day, my beloved will return to me. I do not say this with any sorrow, for I love the radiant flow of each day. Yet recently I've been awakening and hearing footsteps in the forest, as if twigs are being stepped on and cracked by a young boy. One day, when my beloved is ready, he will return, and on that day, under a radiant sun, a new era will begin. It will be a time when each man remembers that to love his woman is to love all of life. Then, and only then, will the Golden Age truly begin. When Codal returns to me, we will love and celebrate this Earth and all that lives upon her. Listen! Sometimes he walks in the forest. I think I hear him coming now ...

Healing with Aine

Finding Aine
Goodness & Radiant Health

As an archetype Aine is the embodiment of goodness and radiant health. When we look for her, we are seeking what is good, bright and true within our own nature. When we access our True Nature, we shine with radiant health and wellbeing.

Known as a Summer or Solar Goddess, Aine is honored on Summer Solstice or Litha, which is traditionally celebrated on June 21, the lightest day of the year. In ancient times, the day was celebrated by making bonfires with bales of hay, known as balefires. The fires were said to drive out negativity and invite in fertility. Some people would peer into the crackling fires and read the future.

Litha Ritual

To connect back to the ancient light of Aine, take dried grasses and light a fire in her honor. Stare into the flames of the fire and allow yourself just to gaze—without thought or agenda—into the Light.

You may ask that the Light burn brightly within you and your loved ones, making you wholesome, healthy, and strong. Peer into the fire and allow your mind to drift. Feel the warmth of the fire and how the heat can befriend and nurture us.

Then close your eyes and turn your focus within. There is an Inner Light that always burns within us, and no matter what happens, this inner flame will never go out. Instead, it will move with us from lifetime to lifetime without changing—for it is the eternal part of our True Nature. Remember to send a spark of your own light to the sun and thank it for always rising. Ask that Aine bless you to be in correct relationship with all inner and outer fires.

Aine in Nature
Oak, A Red Mare, & Yellow Blossoms

We can remember Aine every day the sun shines upon us. We can feel close to her every time we light a fire or a candle, and be reminded of the eternal flame that always burns within us. She understands the spark of life that exists within all sentient beings, including animals, flowers, and trees. The unassuming skylark with a most beautiful voice may be Aine inviting us into a sunny meadow.

Aine can also appear to us in Nature as a Horse, Oak tree, Daisy, Sunflower, or Grain. When the horse comes to you in a dream or a vision—particularly a Red or Chestnut Mare—remember that your personal power is related to the ability to view events from a higher perspective. When you encounter an Oak tree, remember that the Druids have honored Oaks for thousands of years. The Druids viewed these trees as symbols of wisdom and revered them for their ability to endure.

When you see a Daisy growing in a meadow, check inside yourself and see if Aine is sending a message about staying balanced and connected to your Inner Light. Daisy *(Bellis Perennis)* Flower Essence is used to keep a hero or heroine grounded and centered, even when the world around seems chaotic. Sunflower blossoms actually follow the sun, and they remind us to follow the Light also. The Sunflower *(Helianthus Annuus)* Essence can help us shine with courage and confidence.

Aine's Colors
Russet, Gold, & Yellow

Aine's three sacred colors are Russet, Gold, and Yellow, colors of the harvest that sustains life. Russet or Reddish Brown is a color that can ground and stabilize. It is a color to wear when we need to come back down to Earth and feel comfortable in our bodies.

When we consciously connect with the color Gold, we can begin to tap into the endless layers of the earth's wisdom that animates all living things. It also activates our personal brilliance. Gold helps us become disciplined, so we can put our innate wisdom to good use.

Yellow is the color of curiosity, laughter, independence, and intelligence. Yellow sunflowers and other yellow flowers—such as buttercups and daffodils—remind us to laugh, play, and enjoy life. Aine inspires us to awaken the ancient Wise One within and become increasingly curious about the world in which we live. This combination of colors is called "Abundant Harvest."

Meeting the Goddess Aine

The fiery Solar Goddess Aine reminds us of our bright knowing, recognized in Welsh as the *glefiosa* (pronounced "glay fee'sa"). Meeting the Solar Goddess reminds us of our Inner Knowing or *gnosis*. Aine is linked eternally to the flame that always burns in the heart of Creation, and so she is independent and needs no one in order to connect to the Infinite Light. Aine can inspire us to develop our own direct knowing and trust the wisdom of our bodies, hearts, and minds.

It takes an evolutionary leap in order for us to claim full responsibility for the life we are constantly co-creating. Once we realize our brilliance, we may start to engage quite differently with each other and the world. Although we may not remember, each of us carries our own unique Light that moves with us from lifetime to lifetime without changing. Our Inner Light is as brilliant as a star or sun that burns eternally.

When asked, Aine initiates us into our own unique brilliance. When we connect with her solar energy, it is as though her flame ignites the wick of a light that already burns within us, and our natural intelligence is invited to awaken to the next level. Intelligent heroes and heroines act according to their own Truth and Inner Guidance. It takes courage to open our hearts to another, even the Great Goddess who gives us life. Yet it is time to tap into the ancient source of wisdom once again, so that the Earth and all sentient beings can thrive. Like Aine, each of us can choose to be a Light upon the world. Are you brave enough to live from your own bright knowing?

Practice
Playing with the Light

In folklore, it is believed that Aine could heal and that she possessed the gift of regulating the spark of life. Every day, the sun shines upon us, which means that Aine is always blessing us with her presence. It is life-affirming to go outside and breathe the Light of the sun into your physical form. When you breathe in the Light, you become more like the Light.

Practice beginning each day aligned with the ancient intelligence of the Light. Each morning at sunrise (or upon waking), practice interacting with the Bright Knowledge. Go outside and feel the Light of the sun as it touches your body, mind, and spirit. If it is cloudy, then light a candle and gaze at the flame. Pull the Light of the fire into your body. You might begin to feel the Infinite Light—the Source of which we are all a part. Notice as you meditate on the Light that it begins to play with you. Breathe in the Light so that each cell of your body is infused with life-affirming energies.

When you are connected to the flow of wisdom, life becomes fun, interesting, successful, healthy, and full of miracles. Blessed are the ones that receive the Bright Knowing, for they are guided through each and every day.

Visualization
Flying on the Red Mare

It is time to voyage to an ancient land to meet Aine, the Solar Goddess who celebrates the Light that shines within you and the spark within all creatures that live. Sit by your Goddess Altar or a sacred place where you will not be disturbed. Close your eyes and place your hands on your belly center. Take three deep breaths and sense the Light of the inner star in your belly — the Incarnational Star. Allow your spirit self to stand up out of your body and prepare for a Quest of Fire.

A portal of spiritual fire appears and a red mare steps through the flames and stands before you. Aine's horse, Lair Derg, approaches your spirit-self carefully, giving you time to sense her great presence. As she gazes upon you with her large, dark eyes, you realize that this mare knows your past, present, and future. She accepts you exactly as you are in this moment.

Kneeling beside you, the mare offers to take you to the Other-worlds. As you slip onto her back, notice that her coat is short and sleek. Lair Derg is a mare that comes to you from a world in which it is always summer. You wrap your hands into her long red mane, and then she lifts off, carrying you up into the sky.

Flying toward the sun, you realize that you are supported in your Quest. You travel through the Light of the sun, which is life-affirming and cleansing. The colors of gold and yellow touch your body as you soar through time and space.

Suddenly, you enter a world that is vibrant and filled with life. Embrace the colors, shapes, and sounds of this Otherworld as Lair Derg spirals downward to a new land.

The red mare lands carefully and takes you to a sacred oak-grove. Notice that the trees are filled with skylarks, and that Faery-folks have gathered to greet you. They are excited that you have come. After you dismount, one of the Faeries places a wreath of daisies and sunflowers around your neck. The Faeries giggle as they lead you up a hill where a fire has been lit. You notice that there is something magical about the flame, that it ignites a spark that also burns within you.

Once you reach the top of the hill, the Goddess Aine steps out of the flame to greet you. She is six feet tall, strong, and has piercing green eyes. You bow to her, honoring the brilliance of her being. Taking a sunflower, she gently taps the crown of your head, and you feel diamond lights radiating from the top of your head. Aine laughs, and you notice how wonderful you feel—how whole and complete. For a moment, you might feel as though you have become the sun.

Aine has a special treasure for you. Holding out your hands in the form of a cup, you request that your Grail be completed by her. The Goddess smiles at you. Aine then brings out a gift that is what you need at this time in your life, and she places it gently in your open hands.

The red mare neighs, and you know it is time to ride back to surface Earth. You turn once again to acknowledge the flame that always burns in the Otherworld. Know now that you are connected to a Light that will always sustain and support you.

Lair Derg kneels and you mount her once again. As the red mare flies up above the sacred hill, you wave to the Faery-folk and the sacred Goddess Aine. Passing through the portal of the sun, you return with all that you need for your health and healing.

The mare lands by your physical body, and your spirit-self dismounts. Thank the red mare for taking you to Aine. Step back inside your physical self and stretch, so that your body, mind, and spirit reunify with the light-filled mandala that is your True Self.

Aine's Goodness Blessing

May you recall your innate goodness

And the light that shines within you.

Each time a ray of sunlight touches you

Remember to share your magnificence

With those who can celebrate you.

Even as the sun dips behind the mountains

Disappearing from our external view,

Notice the fire still lit in your heart.

The blessing of the Goddess is eternal.

SCATACH

Scatach in Celtic Myth & Legend
Scotland's Warrior Goddess

S catach is a Goddess of the Ulster Cycle, one of the four grand cycles of Celtic mythology. In the 1st century BC, she was known as a warrior woman and martial artist who made her home in the northwest of Scotland on the Isle of Skye or *Dun Scaith*, which means "cloud island." Her residence is known as the Fortress of Shadows. Some claim she is still there instructing those who dare to dream of becoming heroes or heroines.

Perhaps she has sweetened over the years, but in her era, any man who wished to find the Warrior Goddess had to cross a perilous bridge over a deadly, twenty-two-foot ravine. The bridge was known as *Droichet na ndaltae* or the Bridge of the Cliff. If a man survived the crossing, Scatach would be standing in front of him, reading his future. He would have one of three destinies. She would either see that he was not cut out to be a hero and kill him, or she would find him attractive and seduce the man—or she would train him to be one of the most feared heroes of the land.

Known as the Shadowy One, Scatach possesses many faces, including that of the sacred one. She has a sister by the name of Aoife and a daughter named Uathach, although it is possible that these are three faces of the same Goddess. If you need strength to face or overcome challenges, she is a co-walker to call upon.

Cuchulain in Myth & Legend
Ireland's Hero

Cuchulain had a supernatural beginning. His mother, Dechtire—the daughter of the Goddess Maga and a Druid—was visited on her wedding night by the Sun God Lugh, who appeared in the form of a fly. The fly impregnated her when she swallowed it. Dechtire gave birth to Setanta, who became known as Cuchulain.

This demi-sun-god possessed many powers, even in childhood. From the time of his birth, Cuchulain could swim like a fish. He was dangerous when enraged. At the young age of seven, he fought off more than one hundred boy warriors in order to enter his uncle's court. When he was twelve years old, Setanta accidentally killed the ferocious white hound of the metalworker Cullan. He offered to guard Cullan's property until another watchdog could be trained. It was at that time that he was re-named Cuchulain, meaning "hound of Cullan."

Cuchulain became a warrior in the King of Ulster's court. He grew to be a handsome, well-spoken man who was very popular with women. When it was time for the hero Cuchulain to wed, the men of Ulster searched all over for a suitable wife for him. However, he was only interested in marrying the great Irish beauty, Emer.

After expressing this wish, Cuchulain was sent to the Warrior Goddess Scatach by Emer's father, the Chieftain Forgall Manach. Forgall hoped the Goddess would kill his daughter's suitor and that Emer would then marry into royalty. But Scatach recognized that the young man was meant to have a short but meritorious destiny, and she decided to train him as a great warrior. His famous rages did not disturb Scatach, who knew an even greater wrath.

Scatach sent Cuchulain back to Emer as a man ready to claim his wife and step into the life of a true hero. We have noted that, in some myths, Scatach has a sister or rival named Aoife. Some legends say these are three separate women, while others describe them as just different faces of the same Triple Goddess. In this version of the tale, Aoife is the loving aspect of Scatach.

Scatach Speaks
Ireland's Missing Tale

Men should learn to attune to their destiny and adhere to it. Many bones of potential heroes rest here under my bridge. Most of these men bored me because they wished for what they could never have. Any true hero knows to stay vigilant for signs, and I send many signs before watching the pretenders stumble and fall like lemmings off a cliff. Few now dare to set foot on my land without invitation, for they fear that I will kill them. My name is Scatach and I am the Warrior Woman of the Isle of Skye.

I can read a man's future, even when he is a hundred miles away thinking that he would like to battle me. Even now they seek me, hoping I will teach them the way of the spear, blade, staff, and rope. They focus too much on material objects and forget the world of spirit, which is where I send them. I can still teach men who perished and live on the other side as ghosts. Their early demise teaches them to be quick-witted, and they return in their next incarnations stronger than before. I connect men to the Light, but often in ways they did not expect.

I live the way of the shadowy Goddess, long since wiped out and forgotten. Some have called me evil, but I am a pristine protector of the Truth. A real warrior stomps on the heads of demons. Our role as Goddess is to maintain the balance of life, uphold justice, and to fulfill our destiny. To do so, we learn the subtle arts, always working in harmony with the natural world.

There was one who was meant to come to me. I watched the handsome youth as he approached the Bridge of the Cliff that leads to my fortress. This is a magical bridge covered in prickly Blackthorns, and it is designed to protect me. Most men who attempt to cross are thrown to their death. As Cuchulain gazed steadily at the bridge, his seven-pleated crimson cloak, held together by a golden brooch, lifted in the breeze for a moment like the wings of a red eagle.

The first time Cuchulain tried to cross, the bridge bucked like a wild bull, sending him reeling backwards, and he tumbled back to where he had begun. He dusted off his fine cloak. Perhaps it was the sun reflecting off his cloak, but his blond hair seemed to fill with red light as he began to grow angry. Still, the enchanted bridge did not fear him, and the next time he tried to cross, it threw him to his knees. I laughed and almost turned away from the boy who wished to be a hero. The third time Cuchulain attempted to cross, the golden light of the Sun God Lugh began to radiate through his eyes and all around him. He steadied himself and, with two long leaps, Cuchulain had crossed the Bridge of the Cliff.

Now he had my attention. I had known Cuchulain was tracking me as soon as Forgall Manach sent him to me to be killed. The old warrior hoped that his daughter would choose a more noble man. Yet it was not for me to take Cuchulain's life, but rather to give him life. He came because he wished to win the hand of Emer, the paragon of Irish women. I not only needed to hone his skills as the greatest warrior in the land, but also help him become the greatest lover. I am skilled in both arenas.

The day Cuchulain made his two salmon-leaps, I was waiting for him. With the skill of a mighty stag, he had jumped, hitting the middle of the bridge and then landing at my feet. I stood poised, ready for the fight, but I did not kill him. I had long known this man was destined to be the greatest hero that Ireland had ever seen. Cuchulain was a forceful youth, and I enjoyed watching him twist and turn as he tried to defeat me. In the beginning, he was no match—but in the end, he was nearly my equal. Cuchulain would never have been able to defeat me and win the island, however, because there were a few secrets I never shared. He had never mastered walking on air, nor could he manifest weapons, and there are other skills few who are living would comprehend. There was always something up my sleeve.

I refused to tell Cuchulain his future because I knew his life as a hero would be brilliant but short, and that he would kill our son Connal with the deadly spear *Gae Bulga* that came from my hand. It is not for me to question the ways of the great Goddess, but to perform the feats that are required of me. I could not resist my fate. By the time Cuchulain and our son battled, I had already taught Connal the art of transfiguration, and so at his death, he took the form of an eagle and lives on with me still. He is a reminder that I was once honored for the skills of the warrior and that I was loved for being who I am.

When Cuchulain asked if I would train him as a warrior, I laughed and threw him to the ground. The young hound was surprised that my petite form had such power. You see, our real strength does not come from our body but from our ability to contact our astral strength. When we do this, we can move beyond the limits of our physical constraints.

Cuchulain mastered some of this instruction, but his heart was turned to his love for Emer and concern for the destiny of Ireland. He wished to be a brilliant flame, and so he was. His story is so fabulous that it has been re-told for thousands of years. Know that there is a hero or heroine living within each of us, and realize that most of the demons that we must overcome are no farther than our own flesh and blood.

Many legends tell of the golden apples that heroes seek in order to reach immortality. They are talismans of good fortune that must be found in the Otherworlds. The feats that Cuchulain underwent during his training with me have been kept secret, but I can share some of what he endured, for it may help you overcome your own shadows. The first involved the magical silver apple tree that bears both silver and golden fruit. If you cut an earthly apple in half, you will see a star in the shape of the pentagram. You cannot cut a Golden Apple of the Sun, for it will turn into rays of light.

The world has become imbalanced by war, intolerance, selfishness, rape, and greed. These are not the ways of the Goddess, and so she must re-awaken within each of us. As I said, in this era, I am a defender of the Truth and one of your dearest allies. When the Goddess awakens within, you will know the sweet taste of the golden apple of immortality, and she will never leave you. When you awaken with the sweet taste of golden apple on your lips, you will know that Tir Na Ban, the Land of Women, is your true home.

When I told Cuchulain that his first task was the apple feat, he roared with laughter and told me that he could find meat in the forest. He boasted that deer would come and lie at his feet for the taking and I knew this to be true. Young bucks wanted to be eaten by him so that they would progress to higher levels and eventually earn the position of warrior.

It surprised him when I said, "If you're such a master, then follow me ..." and then disappeared into the forest. He had not learned to dissolve his form and appear again. He ran through the forest as if in a dream. Cuchulain was furious and turned red, and he was even more startled when I appeared in front of him holding an apple.

"Were you able to follow me?" I asked coyly.

He took a jab at me with his sword, but I was too quick for him. I managed to swipe his broad chest with nails as sharp as cat claws. He hardly flinched, so I sent him a blast of wind from the Underworld that made him shudder with fear. I appeared a hundred feet in front of him and called his name, and he ran toward me with his dagger drawn. I disappeared and appeared again another hundred feet in front of him, and he followed, panting like a good hound. It was an effective game of fetch, and soon I had led him to the apple tree of Skye, which has long since been felled by ignorant hands. Apple trees are sacred and should never be harmed.

I sat in the branches, licking the juice of a golden apple. "You have to climb up the tree to taste the healing fruit," I said. I knew he would need this medicine in years to come when he would step from the body of a warrior into a body of Light. Yet these ideas were beyond the comprehension of a young man.

Every time he tried to climb up the limbs of the tree, it would strike him down with one of its branches. Every time he drew a weapon, the tree would knock it from his hand—until, at last, Cuchulain was bare-handed.

"Naked is how you approach the sacred Goddess," I said. "Later you can warm yourself with clothes."

He looked puzzled for a few moments and then dropped his garments. This time, he approached the tree and knelt. The tree no longer assaulted him but handed him one of her fruits. He held the radiant apple in his hands for a few moments, sniffed it, and then bit it, allowing the juices to flow between his lips and heal his wounds. He became radiant, and I knew that he indeed had the makings of greatness.

I descended from the tree and battled him. Cuchulain was still bound to the Earth. In his nakedness, he was easy to smack, and I enjoyed playing with him in that way. After a while, he realized that the battle was a flirtation. Like the serpent to Eve, I had offered him an apple that he could not resist. I also let my clothes fall away and allowed him to chase me.

When he caught me, I explained that within me lived my twin sister, Aoife, who would always love him, but that Scatach herself never loved a man. He seemed to understand my divided nature and took me in his arms so gently that I melted into him.

But Scatach is a force to be reckoned with, and while Cuchulain slept, she returned within me to fulfill his training. I poured a sleeping potion into his mouth. He tried to spit it out, but the herbs were already entwining him in astral vines. I did this because Cuchulain had to undergo another initiation, one which makes the uninitiated shudder. It is known as the Supine Feat, and he had to be tested in order to face who he was destined to become. After drinking the potion, most men would have spent weeks fighting nightmares. Yet Cuchulain slept for an hour seeming quite relaxed, even though his dreams must have been filled with horrors.

Exhausted and spent, Cuchulain had been off-guard as he slept next to my twin-self, Aoife. My Aoife and Scatach selves have long been enemies, because Aoife wishes for things Scatach can never have. I did my best to silence Aoife, but Cuchulain's love helped my sister-self and I find peace and inner reunion. I never told him how he healed the inner divide that had split my psyche for so long. In truth, Cuchulain was a healer and lives on even now to help those who need to conquer their inner madness. In this way, he has become a true and everlasting hero.

My warrior-self awakened Cuchulain with a dagger at his throat. "I could kill you," I said. "Your guard is down."

He opened his eyes in a relaxed fashion, and at first thought I was playing with him, until I pressed harder. Cuchulain realized that I had bound him in the cobwebs of my desire and that my poison could overcome him. He struggled to free himself but could not. Even his famous rage and growing strength could not free him from my grip.

"There is a secret," I said. "But it does not come from strength." He flapped like a trapped bird. I cut him just enough to make a slow trickle of blood run from his neck. "An enemy would already have your head, and might one day, if you aren't careful. If it happens, call me, and I will teach you the raven's flight. But not until you are a spirit."

Cuchulain let out a mighty roar that scared the seabirds, who took flight. I laughed and told him that the hero's yell was something that I might teach him later, if he survived the day.

"King Lugaid wants your beloved Emer as his wife," I taunted. "Can you see the union that Forgall wishes to form? He wants his daughter to awaken in a king's bed, and she will—but not amongst the pillows that he suspects." I then laughed, but Cuchulain snarled.

"I will have his head if the King touches Emer," he said, turning so red that I thought his blood might boil.

"I will lay a curse on any king now that if he so much as touches a hair on your head, he will lose his hand and kingship," I told Cuchulain. Did I actually curse his enemy, or simply tell Cuchulain what was to come that day at Knockbridge when he would make his last stand, when his grey mare would lie beside him and weep tears of blood? Sometimes, knowing the future would only weaken you, so I left the vision suspended in time, awaiting its own unfolding. It was time for life, not death, so I kissed his lips just for fun while he struggled. I bit him, too, just so Cuchulain knew I was his master.

"You're in the grip of magic," I said. "No one and nothing can free you but yourself."

"I am surely doomed," he said.

"With that attitude, yes," I said flippantly. "A hero must never, for one moment, imagine defeat, for that only pulls the possibility in closer. A hero must learn the power of his own magic."

I left him to struggle in the web of the Goddess.

When I returned at dusk, Cuchulain had stopped struggling and was resting quietly. I sat beside him and knew that he was not sleeping but becoming aware of a greater presence.

"What do you see?" I asked him.

"I see that I am a puppet in the hands of the Goddess" he said, "and she is toying with me."

"Have you surrendered to her will?" I asked.

"I surrender to the will of no one!" he said boldly, perhaps too boldly for one in his position.

I left him there that night for the wild animals to sniff. Never was I far away, but Cuchulain had no way of knowing whether he had been entirely abandoned. Once or twice I heard him call out, and perhaps he wept for the young boy that died within him that night. I am not cruel, but a warrior does not survive if fear can paralyze him. He must be purified so that he can face any situation without flinching.

In the morning, I sat by him once again and asked, "And now do you surrender to the will of the Goddess?"

"I see that she gives and takes life; that without her, our bodies are but an empty husk," he said. "I surrender to the will of the Goddess and the greater eternal Light that never fails."

He had mastered the Supine Feat, for the nightmares of his own imagination did not break him. It is one of the most frightening tests any warrior ever undergoes, because the personality is destroyed and the shining Light of pure essence replaces it.

"Connect yourself to the Great Goddess and the Light of eternal youth," I said. "Never know any fear from this time forward, and arise as the shining sun of Ireland." I placed the strength of the hero into his middle finger, where he might always find it. Then I directed, "Take your middle finger and free yourself from all that binds you."

He lifted his left hand and the cords that bound him vanished. Finally free, Cuchulain lay on the ground for a few moments. Then the Great Goddess was in front of him, shining, radiant, and beautiful. She had taken on the form of Fand, the most beautiful creature of the Faery realm. He was mesmerized for a moment, and I saw that one day, Cuchulain would love her as he had loved me. But for this short time, he would be mine, and that was enough.

The Goddess shifted from the beautiful maiden Fand to the swollen image of mother and smiled at him. "You must be the protector of women if you serve me," she said. "Remember not to harm your son. You will recognize him by his ring."

Cuchulain slowly sat up and said, "I am yours and I will do what you ask."

Then she turned into the form of Cailleach, the Hag Goddess with a blue-grey face and one eye, and said, "Never eat the flesh of a hound, for if you do, that will be the day you will leave this life. Also, don't refuse hospitality."

She laughed and then shifted into the shadowy Goddess of Death. Drawing back her veil, the Crone smiled, showing a few crooked teeth. Her head was bald and one eye was cloudy, but the other was piercing. The Hag can horrify the most ferocious warrior. I've seen many men drop to their knees and weep, for they see that in front of her, they are as helpless as a baby.

Cuchulain stared into her single eye without flinching. Satisfied that there was no fear in him, she left in the form of a crow.

There was soon a loud crack of thunder, and I knew Cuchulain would be required to accomplish the Thunder Feat next. A storm blew in and a fierce wind began to blow across the island. The day darkened and a thick mist blocked out the sun. Lightning struck the stone near Cuchulain, who stood up, glowing. The lightning was drawn to him, and everywhere he went, long shafts of light hit the earth, cracking boulders and sending smaller stones scattering.

At last, he grabbed a spear and held it skyward. The next bolt touched his weapon, and the jolt of electricity knocked him backwards. Cuchulain had the juice of the golden apple in his veins, and so he stood again and became the lightning rod of Skye. He was struck again and again with such force that I almost cried out to the Goddess for mercy. He stood against a rock and took these activations without a whimper.

With each lightning strike, he resisted less, until finally he and the lightning were one. The thunder rolled and the storm began to move out toward the sea. As the sun rose in the early morning light, I could see that he still stood. Cuchulain had been blackened by the ordeal, but was still alive—perhaps more alive than ever before.

"The Great Goddess must have tremendous plans for you," I said, appearing before him. I noticed then that his eyes were different. They had none of the gentleness from our lovemaking, but the intensity of a great hero.

The rains came that morning and bathed Cuchulain as he learned to walk again with the fire and thunder that now lived and breathed inside of him. From then on, lightning would be part of who he was as a man and hero.

We made our way to the healing lake, where Cuchulain was re-formed and re-newed. This time the healing was gentle, and the Ladies of the Lake bathed his blond curls, kissed him, and reminded Cuchulain that he was still a man.

Cuchulain spent a year with me. I taught him to use his great salmon-leap from a chariot, which made him a ferocious opponent, and many other secrets that must not be shared. They are only revealed to heroes and heroines whose time has come. For the uninitiated to know what cannot be revealed would surely cause harm.

To test his strength, Cuchulain battled me for my island, but after several weeks, he realized he could never defeat me. I did not have it in my heart to kill him, for I was now carrying our son, so I made myself almost impossible to find. I tortured him with dark visions and every kind of sorcery, but I was just playing with him. I never told Cuchulain what life moved within me, because he had his destiny to live out and I had mine.

After many days of fighting, I brought out the hazelnuts of wisdom and sat with him, recounting our days together. Ancient wisdom flowed into him as soon as he tasted the nuts, and he understood the year of training. Finally, when he was ready, I gifted Cuchulain with the *Gae Bulga*, a great, barbed spear that, when thrown with the foot, could slice through any flesh. It was with this weapon that Cuchulain would be known, but the already-wise knew him from his Light that flashed like the sun on a hot afternoon.

"When I came here, I thought I was to become a hero," he told me. "And I wished to win Emer's hand. But now I realize that I came here because it was my destiny. There is no self to battle, no hound that must achieve, but a destiny to live into which has already been designed by the Goddess. A peace fills me now, and in many ways, I could stay here with you battling and loving in the ways of the shadowy one. However, it is not what I am called to do. If I did stay here, my days would be cut even shorter, because this is not where my path leads."

"You must go to Forgall now and claim your bride, Emer," I said. The Goddess had kindly wrapped me in a protective cloak of neutrality, and I was grateful for that as I spoke those words. No tears would be shed that day, and not until his Light and warmth were far from my land did I weep. Once he was gone, I would dig a well to hold my tears.

"To claim Emer," I said, putting heather blossoms in his curls, "you will need to use the Salmon Feat of the Chariot Chief. Forgall will challenge you, and to win Emer, you must use all your strength. That feat will be your first test. If Emer agrees to love you and become your wife, and the Druid Chief Cathbad marries the two of you, your short life will be filled with Light and great achievements."

"Is there anything else you see for me, great sage?" he inquired, with complete reverence. I sensed how he had shifted, and how knowing him had also transformed me.

"Many things are best left unsaid," I replied, reviewing his life and knowing that I would never see him in this world again. "As long as you listen to and align with the Goddess, as long as you honor nature, as long as you love your woman, your life will be blessed. If you defile the feminine, however, your life will be cursed," I warned.

"I will honor the ancient ways and I am one with them," declared Cuchulain. "The lessons of the Goddess are one with me now, and you have made me whole."

"Then go in peace," I said. "May we meet again when the veils are thin and our bodies are made of Light."

Cuchulain kissed my forehead and I allowed it. Then he handed me a red-gold ring and said, "If I have fathered a son, tell him to wear this ring so that I can recognize him."

Cuchulain turned and made his way to the Bridge of the Cliff. When the magical bridge bucked, it did not unsteady him, and he jumped across as easily as the Ireland's magical Salmon of Wisdom.

Driving Cuchulain's chariot, Laeg soon arrived to collect the hero. The chariot was pulled by the warrior's loyal grey mare, Liath

Macha, who would be with Cuchulain to the end, and the mighty black stallion, Dub Sainglend. The hero nodded to acknowledge Laeg and leapt into the chariot, ready to fight the great battles that were to come. He did not look back but drove toward his future, his wife, and his bright destiny. Yet he was within me then, stirring in the form of a child, and I was more within him than he would ever know.

Healing with Scatach

Finding Scatach
Strength, Rigor & Discipline

As an archetype Scatach is the embodiment of strength, rigor and discipline. When we look for her, we are seeking the strength and discipline we need to live long, healthy and successful lives.

Scatach is honored on December 2, as a Goddess who teaches heroes and heroines the arts of living and dying. It is a day to honor the gift of prophecy and to spend time contemplating our life purpose and mission. Scatach can be called upon during Samhain celebrations (October 31 – November 2), for she helps the initiate see clearly into the future. Scatach does not flinch in the face of life or death, and she embraces the totality of the moment. When we are fully present, we stand in our power with the ability to create Heaven on Earth.

The Warrior Goddess is now increasingly understood and honored in western culture. We realize that this feisty archetype is a necessary part of a healthy and thriving psyche. Scatach's essence of strength can be called upon when boundaries need to be set.

Scatach in Nature
Ravens, Apple Blossoms & Silver Bells

In order to find a doorway to the Blessed Isle, you may need to watch to see where the Ravens fly and Faeries play. It may be at the edge of a stream or along the seacoast or by a standing stone or cave. Often it is by a thicket of Blackthorns, trees that protect wise women and magical folk. She can sometimes be found where Apple Blossoms drift between worlds.

Scatach is also a guardian of the Faery Tree with Silver Bells that bears both silver and golden apples as well as pears. In order to fully know ourselves, we need to find our place of retreat and learn to turn within. If you sit at the base of an apple tree and hear bells, know that the Spirits from another world are calling to you.

Scatach's Colors
Indigo, Red, & Violet

The three colors sacred to fiery Scatach are Indigo, Red, and Violet. When used correctly, this dynamic color combination connects the Otherworlds and Earth. It also helps protect the Grail seeker from negativity and danger.

Indigo activates abilities that are beyond the range of the normal five senses. The color stimulates innate clairvoyance (clear seeing), clairsentience (clear sensing), and clairaudience (clear hearing) in the Grail seeker. Those who are innately intuitive may develop the gift of prophecy.

Red is the essence of strength that heroes and heroines need for their Quest. Some people resist the color because, as a distorted energy, Red is anger. When used correctly, it activates the rising kundalini and is healing for the body. It can also be expressed as action. When Red is evoked as an essence, you might feel the strength of a dragon living within your body. It is the color that awakens the initiate to non-ordinary states of consciousness.

The Violet flame is used for healing and transformation. It is a spiritual color that can restore peace and harmony within the body, mind, and soul. When we heal, seven generations are healed in both the past and future. Violet can activate the seventh sense, our ability to see into the future, and also clear negative energies so that life can flourish.

These three colors combine to support a person in guarding the mysteries that only initiates know and, because it stimulates the sixth and seventh senses, it is known as the combination of "Prophecy."

Meeting the Goddess Scatach

The role of the Goddess Scatach is to test the potential hero or heroine. Inner strength is related to the color Red, and when the essence of strength is awake in you, then you have what it takes to continue the Quest. If you have not integrated your Red essence, you will be tested until you stand in your Truth.

Meeting the Goddess Scatach will challenge you. She will teach you boundaries and to honor the word NO. If you are still identified with fear, she will try to throw you off your path. Scatach might come in the form of a Goddess, but she often shape-shifts into something you were not prepared for, such a Raven, or even a nightmare.

Be present and mindful, because she might appear in your life as a person who shouts at you for no apparent reason, or in the form of a reckless driver who makes you swerve at the last moment. Another one of her favorite tricks is to appear as an illness that you have to fight. Alternately, your partner might accuse you of something that seems outrageous, or a friend might do something that you regard as completely unjust and unfair. If so, check to see if Scatach is working through them. Perhaps she is seeing if you have what it takes to be a hero or heroine.

Scatach can take you to your knees if you're not prepared for her. But if you are wise, then you will recognize her. In actuality, she is your greatest ally. If someone shouts at you, just smile and walk away. If you need to veer suddenly when you are driving, do so and keep going. If you're accused unjustly, then align with your Truth. Stay attuned to the present moment, but also be aware of what the future holds. The Quest is a test, and you must be prepared for anything.

Practice
Being Present with the Living Landscape

Every day upon rising, be conscious of the gift of your body that has been renewed by sleep and dream messages from the Otherworlds. Take time to connect to the sunlight and to the intelligence that resides within you. Then, as you rise, make certain that you honor all aspects of Nature: spirit, fire, air, earth, and water. Your body arises as part of the living landscape. You are part of all that is.

Visualization
Leaping Across the Enchanted Bridge

Visualize yourself standing on the edge of Scatach's ravine on the mystical Isle of Skye in Scotland. There is a mist that holds you with great love, for you need the strength of the Goddess for this next stage of your journey to wholeness. See your feet on the rocky surface. The heather and gorse are blooming with pink and yellow flowers. Feel that their essence naturally empowers your body. Perhaps this is the best your physical form has ever felt! In this moment, you have the courage of a true hero or heroine.

When you're ready, leap across the enchanted Bridge of the Cliff and be prepared to meet the Goddess Scatach. This Goddess knows your future, and she is also powerful enough to re-align it.

As you leap through space, time slows down and you experience your own life review. The suffering, pain, betrayals, hurts, or self-judgments that no longer serve you can now be released to the bottom of the ravine. A mighty river flows amongst the rocks far below and the water can carry hurts or grievances out to the sea for recycling. It is important to let go of everything that does not serve you, for anything that weighs you down can interfere with the success of your journey. Look ahead, let go, and see yourself landing deftly on Scatach's isle.

The wise Goddess Scatach is waiting for you. She peers with great intensity into your eyes. Even before you have landed, she has read your future. She smiles and offers you the tools that you'll need for your journey to wholeness. Perhaps she gives you a healing herb such as a Thistle, or a cauldron filled with magical red, indigo, and violet lights (for these are her sacred colors). Or perhaps she hands you a golden apple for healing, or a weapon you can use to defend your personal Truth. You receive exactly the gifts you need at this time. Once you have received them from Scatach, turn back toward the place you came from.

A cloud comes at your bidding and carries you safely to your original time and place. As you feel your newly found courage, know this: *You have what it takes to be completely and authentically yourself.* Feel the strength that fills your body and enjoy your new level of health and vigor. You have passed the test, and you can now continue on your hero's or heroine's journey.

Thank the Goddess Scatach for her generosity and enjoy the gift she has given you. If you call upon her, she will always help you defend your Truth. The gift of courage is yours to protect and keep.

Scatach's Strength Blessing

Strength and rigor are often shunned,

But who can be a hero or heroine without them?

The one who is disciplined can withstand

Times when the sky is grey too long

And loneliness makes you want to howl.

Strength, disciple and rigor encourage us,

Like water around the salmon, to swim upstream

And leap,

Not knowing if the jump will be enough

Yet practicing with faith and hope,

Trusting that some wise force will guide us home.

Strength and rigor are friends when all else fails.

They help us stay present through the night,

Reminding us that dawn will come again.

In the morning light we may see new colors,

Perhaps even those sent from Tir Na Ban,

Where apple trees with silver bells

Shimmer in the eternal light.

The sound from Avalon can offer us strength

And heal our souls of all that ails.

Listen, the bells are ringing even now.

EMER

Emer in Myth & Legend
The Beauty of Ireland

he love story of Cuchulain and Emer, recorded in 700 AD, is part of the Ulster Cycle, a body of largely heroic legends from Celtic mythology. Emer captured the imagination of the great poet W.B. Yeats, as well as Lady Gregory and other writers during the Irish Literary Renaissance. The daughter of a gold trader and *taoiseach* (or chieftain) named Forgall Monach, Emer was a celebrated beauty. It was she who would become the wife of the hero Cuchulain, who was the son of Dechtire, sister of Conchobar mac Nessa, King of Ulster.

Having heard descriptions of her great beauty, Cuchulain visited Emer at Forgall's fortress in County Dublin, and he wooed her with his words. He had been loved by many women, but Emer took him by surprise. As he spoke with her, his heart opened in a way Cuchulain did not expect, and he knew with the certainty of a warrior that he had found his wife.

Emer was practical and would not be swept off her feet immediately, saying she would accept Cuchulain as a husband only when he had proven he was ready for the position. Emer's father Forgall was opposed to the marriage. Hoping to kill off the suitor, he suggested that Cuchulain go and train with the Scottish sorceress Scatach, who was on *Dun Scaith*, the Isle of Skye. While Cuchulain was away, Forgall was determined that Emer should marry royalty, and he offered Emer to Lugaid mac Noís, a king of Munster. However, when the King heard that Emer had promised herself to the young hero Cuchulain, Lugaid thought it best to refuse her hand.

Emer was said to have been given six gifts that made her shine like a gentle sun: beauty, a gentle voice, sweet words, quiet wisdom, chastity and the ability to weave beautiful and magical tapestries. Our story begins at the first meeting of the two young lovers at Forgall Manach's fortress, Luglochta Loga, the gardens of Lugh.

Emer Speaks
Ireland's Missing Tale

Even while protected within the walls of my father's kingdom, I had heard wild tales about a young hero. The ladies of the court whispered that he was from the north, and that when he fought, there was a supernatural Light that would protect him. This did not surprise me since his father was the Sun God Lugh, the Shining One, who had quested and obtained the three golden apples of the Hesperides and other magical items. What I knew of Cuchulain made him sound fierce, and at first, I dreaded making his acquaintance. Over time I learned that women had nothing to fear from him, for he was both a warrior and a lover.

We lived in unsettled times and there were constant raids by bands of restless men. I understood my mother's otherworldly ways, and knew I would not be harmed. Yet the rites of the Goddess were slipping away like the sand falling through an ancient cairn. It was not a time to walk between worlds, but to live fully in this realm. I knew I would marry because I had been groomed since birth to be the wife of a king or hero.

The ways of men interested me, especially their quick wits and riddles. I loved to run; I also loved to sew, weave and embroider. Since I enjoyed weaving—an occupation that was honored by the men and women of the court—I was free to colorfully express myself in that way. Even so, people did not understand that I could weave magic into my art. I still enjoy the feeling of yarn slipping through my fingers on the loom. Weaving, sewing, and creating tapestries brought me joy throughout my long life, even after the hero Cuchulain left his body. I take the finest webs of Light and play with them, until they become beautiful pieces of art.

The other thing I love about weaving is that as I work I can talk freely amongst women. When I was young, we all dreamt of our husbands. We knew what our mothers had endured and had watched them closely as they keened the deaths of their husbands. Most of these men had died in battle. Some women married again; others moved silently amongst walls of the stone fortress as if they had become ghosts. We knew the dangers of disease and childbirth, and shared the knowledge of the herbs and incantations that would help us during the many phases of our lives. We ladies of the court hoped that these ways of the wise women would not be overlooked or forgotten by our daughters and granddaughters.

Over time, my dreams had begun to shift from the colorful images I wove into my tapestries toward dreams with so much radiance that I began to wonder if the Sun God Lugh was visiting me in my sleep. I never spoke of this inner radiance to anyone, but I assumed I was being prepared for someone special. On my 16th birthday, a dream began to visit me in which I was looking into eyes that were as blue as the Irish sea on a sunny day. At other times, it seemed that I was looking into a cloudless sky at sunrise, watching the burst of the rays of the morning sun spread warmth across our green land. Sometimes I would awaken suddenly after feeling strong arms embracing me. It was a dream, and yet I knew that the touch of Spirit was calling me forward to my destiny.

I would be so energized that in the mornings I would have to walk with my guardians through my father's gardens, and sometimes beyond the safe haven of the great walls. I liked the wild places where flowers suddenly blossomed and the vines climbed over and pulled down stone walls. So special to me were the clover blossoms and shamrocks, for they sent their messages of love and hope in splendid arrays of pink and green through hills and valleys. I loved the small creatures that came to be under my protection. I fed and tended wild birds, rabbits, young deer and kittens. There was something about the sound of purring cats that would put me into a deep reverie, but my favorite of all creatures are the songbirds.

My mother knew the ways of the Goddess well, and since she was married to my father, the powerful Forgall Manach, she knew how to use her womanly enchantments. She taught me how to read messages in the wind so that I could hide long before trouble came. Often, birds were my eyes; I learned to merge with the winged ones as they flew, to survey the land. Then a time came when Mother spoke less and less of our gifts and intuition because an era had arrived when men would rule. Still, we were not as innocent as we seemed. My mother taught me that I could be a great ally to another by being a trusted confidant, and that we lived long when we practiced sweetness and kind words. She also gave me a knife that I wore as a bracelet, and she taught me how and when to use it.

Mother encouraged my beauty to blossom and emerge at its proper time by threading golden silks into my long hair. My elder sister was to marry first, so I sewed a dress for her of the finest linen, to help her attract a man. When a dress is cut in a way that shows just enough breast and skin, a woman becomes irresistible.

I also learned how to contact the Goddess Eriu in visions. When the Goddess responded to me, I could sense her rising up to an enormous height. She would send flowers cascading through the other world into my own. The room would soon be perfumed with the smell of sweet blossoms. She was teaching me how to cast a glamor. I did not realize at first that these were the ways of love.

I knew that women were required to lay with their husbands. Eriu was not advising me to meekly submit to a man, but how to weave sunlight around him so that he would grow warm and content. My mother secretly taught me how to make tinctures and teas that would add to a man's arousal. She whispered words that she said would enchant a man's heart. As I blossomed into womanhood, I knew a man worthy of my status would find me. I need not look, for as bees find their way to flowers, all I had to do was ripen and bloom.

The day Cuchulain came and stood in our garden, I was wearing a deep violet dress that was snug at the waist. He wore a red cape that snapped in the anxious breeze and his hair seemed to be lit by the startling rays of an exposed sun. I knew he was staring at me, but I was busy with my weaving and did not turn to meet his gaze. After all, it was my sister who was meant to wed first. I continued to sew sunlight and the perfume of flowers into my tapestries, and also around him.

I did not look at Cuchulain directly, but I saw him in his fullness. He was tall, young, lean and muscular. His blond hair fell down his back in ringlets that only accentuated his manliness. Cuchulain had been hardened by the elements, but he had become one with the air that breathed him. He knew the fire that burned within. The soil that he stood upon was an ally that supported him, and even the streams would begin to flow towards him when he was thirsty. The Earth loved Cuchulain and did his bidding. He was a true hero, and I knew all this without ever turning around to look at him.

I heard the women giggling to try to get his attention. I turned at last and saw that Cuchulain's eyes were burning with passion, as if trying to undress me with his stare.

"So, young hero," I said finally, "I understand that you like riddles."

"I do," he said.

"Do you know why you have come to gaze upon Emer?" I teased. I then turned away, as if I were already bored with him. But the truth was that when I had gazed into his eyes, I felt cold sweat beginning to trickle down my back.

I began to hum in the way I was taught, for it informs and supports the flow of life. I sent the perfume of a thousand flowers into and around him once again.

For a moment, Cuchulain seemed confused. He was used to women who threw themselves at him. That was not my destiny, for I was his match. He knew it and that unsettled him.

"Yes, I have come to gaze upon Emer," he said at last. "For I have heard that she is the most beautiful woman in the land."

The other women began to back away as if feeling the potent heat of the moment.

"And what do your own eyes tell you?" I asked, continuing to sew.

"You are full of riddles," he said. He paused for a moment as if struggling with his thoughts.

Again I cast a glamor around him and watched as the hairs on his forearms rose in response. He turned around for a moment as if looking for some unseen force. Then he turned back, surveying me closely and sniffing the air like a hound. I knew he wanted to touch me. But he could not. Not yet.

"My eyes tell me that all the poets and bards have lied," he said.

He was looking at me with such passion that I could feel it now, and I had to turn and face him. Our eyes locked.

"You are beyond what beauty can describe," he declared.

My breath was becoming shallow, and I had to remind myself to breathe as my pulse increased. Cuchulain came closer until he was just behind me, and I could feel his breath upon my exposed shoulders. He touched my hair gently with his broad hands, running his fingertips like a comb through my curls. It was enough to send shivers cascading through my body.

"You come too close before your time," I said, standing up and facing him.

"Please marry me," he said.

"You know nothing of me," I responded. But I had turned as pink as a morning rose.

"Alas, I know too much of you," he said. "I want you as my wife and no other."

He drew his lips toward mine, and I stepped back slightly and then tripped on the fringe of my long dress. He caught me without effort, and for a moment, I was in the great arms that I had dreamt of. The suddenness of the touch surprised us both. I felt both his great strength and his gentleness.

"It is my father who must approve," I said at last, standing up and then turning away from him. "My sister is supposed to marry first and he will offer her to you, and then me to Lugaid mac Noís." I walked back toward the women, who had grown silent as they stood nearby.

I noticed that Cuchulain's face and body had begun turning red, and his eyes were beginning to exude Light. I found his radiant power disconcerting and seductive at the same time.

"If he gives you to another, the man he chooses will not see the last rays of the day," he vowed.

"You must ask my father for my hand," I insisted. Yet even as I uttered the words, I knew Forgall would refuse to give me to any man less than a king.

"Do you wish to be known for all time as my greatest love?" asked the hero.

"No," I said firmly. "I wish to marry a man who will love, support and protect me throughout my many days. I will have no less of a husband than that." I wondered if this handsome youth was capable of the tasks that lay ahead of him.

At first Cuchulain looked surprised, but I realized that he enjoyed the banter. I was not desperate to be his, at least on the exterior. I felt him run his gaze over my body one last time.

"I shall speak to your father," he told me. "I can perform any feat he wishes in order to win your hand. It is you who must decide if I'm worthy of your love and your bed."

And then Cuchulain departed as suddenly as he had arrived. All the women around me were talking again, but I turned my focus back to my loom. I needed to simply feel into what had occurred.

Several weeks later Cuchulain returned to ask my father for my hand in marriage, but I never saw him. My mother later told me that Forgall had said I was too young and offered my sister to him, and Cuchulain had refused. He told my father that Emer was to be his wife and he would marry no other. Forgall had replied that in order to wed me a man must be a King or a hero. My father added that Cuchulain must undergo a trial before a decision could be reached, and then had sent him to Scatach.

I shuddered hearing these words. I knew the sorceress would either make a hero out of him, or he would die at her hand. I cried myself to sleep that night, and it would be many moons before I saw the hero again.

Cuchulain never told me what happened during the years in which we were separated. As time passed, I wondered if it would be wise to accept the Munster King, Lugaid mac Noís, as my husband after all. But in my dreams I was held in the arms of a radiant sun, and so I refused the wishes of my father and waited.

One afternoon, Lugaid mac Noís came to see me in my waiting room. When he was announced, I was busily working on a tapestry of a rising sun. The King was a large, elderly yet handsome man who exuded power. Finely dressed and wearing perfume, it was clear that his intention was to win me for himself. Although he had won many battles, Lugaid did not bear a scar. The King asked if he could spend some time with me. I turned away from my tapestry and nodded in the affirmative.

I bore Lugaid no ill will, so I sat with him in the courtyard with the intention of earning his friendship and understanding. The spring breeze blew gently along the stones, and although it was the time of year to wed, my heart was elsewhere. Lugaid spoke with me for some time, and I politely returned his attention, engaging in conversation. He was pleasant enough. But when the King began to speak to me of marriage, I told him that I loved Cuchulain of Muirthemne. It was then that Lugaid's countenance darkened.

"I hear the young hero now has taken a lover in the dark forests of Scotland," he told me. "It is said she is heavy with child."

The news was shocking, and I felt a chill pass through me as if shades of darkness were engulfing me from an ancient cave. I wondered how this child might impact my life with Cuchulain. I shook off the vision and did not allow the jealousy to stay with me, for it was only gossip. Still, I felt the truth behind the words.

I watched Lugaid's lips move while I entered the silence of my own inner world. I located Cuchulain with my inner vision, as my mother had taught me when I was a child. He was in a dark forest, and I saw him making great leaps across a bridge over a deep ravine. I could sense that he had faced Scatach after this crossing, but then my inner sight faded into a hazy mist that I could not penetrate.

Clearly, there were secrets I was not to know that were protected by magic. For a moment, I thought I could see Scatach's face and her hands began to cover my eyes. I drew back with a shudder.

"I can offer you protection and my kingdom," said Lugaid. He placed his large and dark right hand on top of my pale left hand. I noticed his ring, gold and covered with polished green gemstones. "I would make a good husband," he added.

I looked at Lugaid for a moment. His face was proud and his green eyes searched mine for an answer. Holding his hand, I could sense into my future with him. Lugaid would be true to his word, and he would love others as kings generally do. I wondered if Cuchulain would be true to his word and return to me, or if he would stay with the sorceress in Scotland.

I closed my eyes and called upon the Goddess Eriu for guidance. I felt entirely neutral as I asked what would happen if I did accept this man. Then a vision came to me so strongly that I almost shrank back with horror. I saw Cuchulain's eyes rolled back and his sword at Lugaid's throat. Blood ran freely across the emerald grass.

"Why do you shudder?" he asked. "Do I offend your gentle nature?"

"I believe you would be a good husband," I said. "But it would evoke the wrath of Cuchulain."

Now I could sense Cuchulain with Scatach. It made my head swim, and I almost wanted to give myself to Lugaid. But again with my inner eye, I saw King Lugaid's face covered in blood. I knew even in another woman's arms, Cuchulain still wanted me and was preparing for our wedding day. After all, he was a warrior and would need a woman in his bed.

"Although other women may love Cuchulain now," I said gently, "he is to be my husband. I do not know this, but sense it to be true."

Lugaid looked at me intently as if he wished to ravish me. I thought for a moment that he might try to steal a kiss from my lips, but then he stood up abruptly. The King bent down and kissed my left cheek roughly, then left the room. I briefly felt sad that I would not know this man, but I sensed a greater destiny waiting.

A few minutes later, there was a commotion in the halls. There was clanging, the dogs howled, and I could hear yelling. The doors to my waiting room burst open and my father entered in a rage.

"I have found a king for you, and you insolently refuse him?" Forgall bellowed. "What do you have to say for yourself?"

I was calm in the face of my father's fury. I knew that though Forgall was powerful, he was not a seer. Still, my father ruled with an iron fist. He forced himself upon my mother and others. He was feared and respected, but I did not flinch in his presence.

"I am promised to another," I said.

I felt a warmth flooding through my chest and the arms of the Goddess around me. I faced my father's rage with openness. And then he hit me. I had not expected it, and I spun backwards and fell to the cold stone floor. Forgall lifted his foot, and then placed it down again. For a moment, I thought he would kick me. I could sense blood filling my mouth. Still prone on the stonework, I sat up slowly. I had never met his rage before this outburst.

"You will marry Lugaid. Do you understand?" he shouted.

"I will marry the man who loves me most," I said, refusing to meet my father's gaze or heed his demands.

"Your hero will never return from the snares of Scatach," he taunted. "She has him twisted around her body even now." He laughed and began to pump his hips. "She knows the secret ways."

Forgall grabbed my hair and pulled me to my feet. I began to hate him then. He pushed me out of the room and toward the main hall where he thought Lugaid waited for me. But I was young and spirited; it was not hard to spin out of his grasp. My father lifted his hand to strike me again. This time, I looked deeply into his eyes and sent him the pink ray of unconditional love. I could feel Eriu around me, protecting me in her web of Light, and he softened.

When we entered the main hall, Lugaid was no longer there. Forgall cried out to his guards, but they said the King had left just before the sun had set.

"Go to your chambers," my father ordered. "I will decide your fate."

I could feel his mind working in ways that could cause harm. To counter his rage, I imagined that he was surrounded by mountains of rose petals. Over time, he did soften, and although we did not speak for several days, my father did not try to harm me again. I continued to weave a web of protection around my beloved Cuchulain. I knew my Light would protect him, and that he needed it as he learned the ways of Scatach.

Spring came, and with it the flowers began to blossom, spreading their sweet scents through the open windows of the fortress. New life was growing, and as the leaves of the young trees unfurled, I could sense that Cuchulain was making his way to me.

I ran up our tower and looked to the north. As the sun made its way across the green hills, I could see horses coming. Within moments, Cuchulain arrived driving a chariot pulled by his horses, Liath Macha and Dub Sainglend. The stallion pranced, awaiting Cuchulain's command. His mare tossed her long, tangled mane. The hero held the reins masterfully and the two horses calmed.

Cuchulain called out my name. He had grown in stature and in strength. His blond hair still fell in ringlets across his muscular body, and my beloved radiated intensity. A raven flew above him and his horses stomped with impatience.

"Emer!" he called out again. "I have returned from Scatach."

My father was soon at my side with his hand over my mouth.

"Do not utter a word," he commanded. "Or you will wish for death."

I could see Cuchulain driving the chariot in a circle. He peered in my direction as though his eyes could penetrate the stones and give him a view of the tower's interior.

I noticed my father motioning for his men to attack. And then I saw a Cuchulain I had never seen. He seemed to grow even larger. His face turned red and he appeared to have eyes all over this body. Within minutes, he had killed 24 men.

A mist began to fill the fortress. Forgall started to drag me down the tower stairs but I resisted, so he pushed me toward the open window. I did not know if my father meant to throw me to my death, but he was a large man and I could not stop him.

"Forgall!" yelled Cuchulain. I could hear him bounding up the stairs. "Face me like a king. Do not hide behind a young woman." His words echoed off the tower walls.

Forgall held my arms and pushed me away from the window. We withdrew into the shadows.

I yelled out to Cuchulain. "I am here, in the tower!"

When Cuchulain entered the room in the upper tower, his eyes had become strangely red. They also bulged, making him appear like an ugly giant. He turned our way as though he already knew where we stood.

Forgall was growing frightened, yet he held on to me.

Cuchulain stood before my father. Perhaps he walked towards us, but it appeared as if he were floating until he got within an arm's distance. Forgall seemed momentarily frozen; was it magic?

And then Cuchulain lifted me out of my father's grasp and pushed Forgall hard. My father stumbled and then I could see the fear in his eyes as he began to fall backwards. I reached out to him, but it was too late. Forgall fell down the cold stone stairs and at the bottom I heard a sickening thud.

As if in a dream, I slowly walked down the stairs to my father. I took his head into my lap and stroked his hair. Forgall opened his eyes and looked at me for a moment.

"Please forgive me," he murmured. "He—the hero—is yours."

A tear ran down my right cheek. Even though he had been cruel at times, my love for my father was stronger than the hatred. He had protected me, fed me and cared for me. I was Forgall's royal daughter and his blood ran in my veins. Sensing that he had passed, I closed his eyes and took a deep breath asking the Great Goddess to take him into her lap.

Cuchulain stood by my side like a great giant. He did not say a word but lifted me up into his arms and carried me to his chariot. I did not struggle with him, for I knew that my destiny was bound with his. No one within the fortress walls made a sound. I noticed my mother watching from a distance, but she never uttered a word as we departed.

Liath Macha and Dub Sainglend pulled us in the chariot across the open countryside. I knew the horses would defend us with hooves and teeth against any enemy. Even though I had seen so much death, I was excited to be with my beloved. Cuchulain began to loosen the belt of my dress.

"You must marry me first," I said. "That was your promise."

Cuchulain looked at me intensely. His eyes were now as blue as an expanse of open sky and as vast as the sea. I noticed that he now had the pull of Mag Mell in him, and that the shadows were already calling him to the hero's Underworld. Scatach had accomplished her work, for he had become the hero-light he sought. He lived his destiny without fear.

And then without warning, he kissed me. It was not what I had expected. I had seen Forgall kiss women, but this was different. When our lips touched, I felt the strength of the sun flood my veins and a powerful life-force surge through me. The intensity of his touch surprised me and I began to shake uncontrollably. He touched my cheek, and his hands grew gentle, then he put a finger on my lips where Forgall had hit me. I began to feel healing flow from his hands. Radiant Light poured through my body once again. I felt as though I was in the warming rays of the sun. The Light was almost blinding, and I started to lose consciousness, but his arms were around me. He placed his hand on my thigh and I knew he could take me.

"You promised," I whispered.

"The Druid Cathbad will marry us tonight," he said. "That is, if you accept me as your husband."

"Yes," I said. "I love you. I accept you. You are my beloved Cuchulain."

Cuchulain looked at me for a long moment, as if reading our future together. Then he raised his hand to my waist.

"I will die young," he said. "But I will be the greatest of all heroes. You will outlive me, but your life will be filled with warmth and comfort even when I am gone. I will see to it."

I leaned into his great form and whispered, "So be it."

He drove his chariot north along a well-worn path that wound through the emerald green fields and hills of Ulster. As the sun set, we passed three sacred trees growing within the reach of one another, the oak, ash and thorn. I knew that although I had left my home, the

Goddess was still with me. We crossed rough earth and went through streams, but the chariot glided smoothly along as if we were flying. Cuchulain's body was radiant with Light, and it warmed me as I slept against his vast body.

"We have arrived," he said, after gently awakening me. I looked out of the chariot to a new world in a new land. The rainstorm, which had soaked us during the night, had ended, and mist filled the damp valley, shrouding the buildings in what seemed to be lace made of clouds. A Druid was standing by the chariot as though he knew that Cuchulain would be showing up soon with his bride.

"This is the woman you choose to be your wife?" the Druid asked Cuchulain.

"She chooses me also," said my hero, stepping down from the chariot and holding his hand out to me. "I love her and wish to have beautiful Emer as my wife and the mother of my children."

"Emer," the Druid said, looking intently at me for the first time. "I am Cathbad. Is Cuchulain to be your husband? Do you willingly choose him for your lifetime companion?"

"Yes," I answered, "I choose him." I was trembling not so much from my rain-drenched clothes, but from excitement. I felt so nervous, and I had to will my body to stand upright beside my beloved as I stepped out of the chariot.

"Then I will perform the handfasting ceremony," he told us. "But there is one condition that you must both embrace."

Cuchulain seemed impatient. "Another delay?" he asked.

"The King, Conchobar, must be offered your bride first," said Cathbad. "It is the custom of the land."

I felt a chill cross my body. "How can that be?" I questioned him.

Cuchulain began to turn red with rage. "Surely he would not ask that of me."

"It is the custom to have the approval of the King. You must be separated until morning and the King will decide," said the Druid.

"I will not wait," Cuchulain told him, walking toward his chariot. He had begun to glow like an Otherworldly sprite. I had the sense that he meant to kill Conchobar.

"Don't be foolish," said Cathbad, stopping him. "The King will want no trouble with you. If he does not sleep with Emer first, others might say that you are King. He cannot risk that. I will speak with him and we will reach a solution."

That night I slept in a strange bed with several women tending me. They took me out of my wet clothes and wrapped me in new finery. I slipped in and out of consciousness, and felt the sunlight entering my body again, as if I were being destroyed and re-made by the power of the Light.

"Emer!" I could hear Cuchulain whispering through the walls, although he was not close.

"Yes," I spoke to him in my mind. We already were living within one another.

"It is settled," he told me. "A compromise has been reached. We must go along with the custom, but you will not be touched. I give you my word."

The marriage ceremony was brief but powerful. Cathbad silently unwound a red cord from around his waist and bound our hands together with it. As he chanted in a language I did not know, I could sense that the Druid was weaving a unique Light around us so that we would become one soul. He wrote strange patterns on my neck and ankles, and then drew on Cuchulain's chest. In some way, I felt that he was preparing me to receive the Light that Cuchulain carried. He also prepared Cuchulain to receive me as a May Queen and High Priestess of the Goddess. The old ways were still alive in me, and I knew I would be strengthened by this union of hero and heroine. I could sense Goddess Eriu near me.

Cathbad also felt her presence, for he nodded in Eriu's direction and then turned to me and smiled.

"You may kiss," the Druid said. "And before you consummate your union, Emer must go to Conchobar and spend the night beside him."

Our hands were still fastened when my husband turned to gaze upon me. Again my body shuddered as I felt his passion, his Light and our future. He raised our still-tied hands up above our heads, tugged against the cords, and drew me into his chest. I felt a surge of power come out of his heart and I sank into his body. His lips were gentle this time, and his actions seemed certain.

"Emer, the most beautiful woman in Ireland, is now my wife," he said. "I will be within you always as a great sun and protector."

"Cuchulain, my beloved husband. You and I are now one soul forever. I am happy to be your wife."

The Druid took out a short knife and severed the cord around our hands. Then he cut a new measure of red cord from around his waist. "Nothing will pass this thread. You have my word," he told us. Cathbad wrapped the fresh cord around my hips.

Cuchulain looked at me for a moment, then turned and walked away. He seemed to disappear into the mist, and I thought for a moment I could hear the music of the Faery-folk.

It was still dark when the Druid Cathbad led me to Conchobar's chamber. The King was in his robes with his body partly exposed. Although he seemed tired, he did not complain. Conchobar was built like a bull, yet I did not fear him.

"You will spend the night in my bed," the King said. He pointed to a luxurious bed covered in fine cloth and large pillows.

I drew back in fright, but Cathbad gently took my hand and also lay on the bed. "Don't be frightened. I will sleep between you, and Cuchulain has my word that no man will touch you. You will be chaste until sunset tomorrow. And then you will be with your husband."

Cathbad was true to his word. The King snored and paid no attention to me. The Druid lay still but did not sleep. I could feel him breathing near me, but neither man dared pass the twine that had been tied around me.

When I awoke, I could see light streaming in through a bedroom window, and that the King had gone. The Druid still lay beside me. I could sense that Cathbad was in another world, even while present in this one. I found it ironic that my father's wish had been granted. I had awakened in a king's bed after all, even if it was not in the way that he had wished.

"He will tell his subjects that you will now be given to Cuchulain," Cathbad told me.

"How is it that a woman can be given like a mare to another?" I asked the Druid. "This is not the way it once was."

"We are entering a time of darkness," he explained, "a time when the ways of the Great Goddess will be understood less and less, and even disappear for a time."

"But the land will despair," I said. "Her colors will fade and Eriu may not come to us at all."

"That is what I see," Cathbad shared. "A new time is coming in which men will rule. And then after time has passed, they will realize their great emptiness. In their despair, they will then seek the Great Goddess once again."

"If the Goddess is betrayed, will she allow them to find her again?" I inquired.

"Eventually," said Cathbad. "Although it may take a thousand years or longer." Then he looked at me and smiled. "Your fate, Emer, is to be loved and respected by all. Your life will be a long and happy one. Today there will be a great celebration! And tonight you will enter the chamber of Cuchulain. Rise and prepare for this sacred day!"

"Cathbad," I asked shyly, "I'm not quite sure what to expect tonight. I do know that Cuchulain has a great Light that sometimes overwhelms me. Yet I feel I am in truth his match. My mother has never spoken about my wedding night with me. There was never time." For a moment, I was sad that my parents would not be able to celebrate my new life with me.

"You have chosen one another, which is the way of love. Cuchulain will know what to do. Once you leave the bedchamber, remember never to speak harshly. Even when angered, it is wise to exchange kind words and maintain a pleasant voice." He looked off into the distance for a moment before continuing. "Your love may only be threatened by a woman of the Sidhe later, much later. If that day comes, do not react with jealousy. Keep a sense of yourself and your husband will return to you. Your love will be brief, and yet it will be remembered for all time."

By now, I was hardly listening, for women had come in to bathe and perfume my body. I was being unwrapped and rewrapped in the finest of silks. They sang a strange song that I did not know, yet it felt deeply familiar.

That afternoon, King Conchobar held a great feast in our honor. I looked around for Cuchulain, but he took his time arriving. I sat next to Conchobar, who I realized had become a trusted friend. Cathbad also sat close by, observing the inner working of the court closely.

At one point, the Druid turned to me and said, "You will be loved by these people and all of Ireland one day. May your goodness stay with you all the days of your long life. You are to be their heroine, the one all women wish to be."

As the last rays of the sun began to fade, Cuchulain strode proudly into the room wearing fine garments. He had bathed and wore perfume. Our eyes met and I felt the fire in my body once again. His hair was bound with golden ribbons and several women led him to the King. He stopped briefly in front of Conchobar and bowed.

Then he walked towards me. It seemed as though the sun had come down from the heavens. I began to burn and sweat. But then, as if in response, I felt a great Light awaken within my belly. The two of us were becoming a great ball of Light. He came to the table and picked me up effortlessly. He carried me out of the room and placed me in his chariot. He never uttered a word. Cuchulain did not need to, because the strength of his passion was clear.

When we arrived in his village, people had lit fires for us and lined a path that had been strewn with flower petals. They all sang the strange Faery song that had worked its way into my heart.

Cuchulain and I walked hand in hand, happily nodding to the people who loved him, and who would grow to love us. When we arrived at the door to his woodland home, my hero stopped and in front of the crowd he kissed me for a third time. Then he lifted me up once again and took me into his chamber as the people cheered.

We had waited for this moment for many years, and now it had come to us as a fine present, ready to be unwrapped. His bed was made of animal furs, and his hound sighed in the far corner of the room as Cuchulain unwound my dress. He took his time, looking very carefully at my body, breathing in the perfume of my flesh. He touched me in a way I had not known before that was both gentle and firm. My body shook with ecstasy, even before he entered me for the first of many times. He was a patient lover, and took his time to please me until at last I grew sore and could not take him any longer. The sun was rising as he roared with his finishing pleasure. His voice shook the stones and rocks, and even the morning chorus of birds grew silent. And then we slept, wrapped around each other like morning glory vines around a living tree.

Our great love was never questioned, and although he left to engage in battle, Cuchulain would always return to me. Except once, but that is another tale, one in which I had to overcome jealousy—as Cathbad had predicted. I have long since forgiven Fand, and Cuchulain has forgotten her. We were married for seven years and I bore him three children, all girls, who were forgotten by history. They all had golden hair with red streaks, and each remained true to herself and found deep love.

On the day Cathbad the Druid came to tell me that Cuchulain had died, I was watching the sun set over the vast Atlantic sea. Taking in the news, I wept. There would never be a man like him again, a radiant sun, a lover to share my bed. As I wept, I felt the touch of spirit and I heard, "Do not despair, my beloved. I live on inside of you."

I touched my swelling belly and smiled knowing that he had chosen his moment well. "Ah, my beloved," I whispered, "we are truly part of one another."

Our love lives on in our children and our family's line of children that span the centuries. If you close your eyes and feel into your heart, you might find that our Light lives on within you also.

Healing with Emer & Cuchulain

Finding Emer & Cuchulain
Beauty & Victory

The Goddess Taillte chose to reside on a mound known as *Temair*, now called the Hill of Tara in County Meath, Ireland. Daughter of Mag Mor and wife of Eochu, she was called Queen of the Fir Bolg. Ordering that the forest be cut down and turned into a field of clover, Taillte activated a powerful vortex on the hill, which would later be recognized as the seat of all the High Kings of Ireland.

In ancient Ireland, Taillte was called the Goddess of August. In folklore it is said she became the Mother of Light, gave the Sun a body so that he could enjoy living on Earth, and named him Lugh. Upon her death, Taillte requested that games be held each year in her honor on the lands she had cleared. Lugh held the first games, which were rather like an early Irish Olympics, and Lughnasa (the Games of Lugh) are still celebrated with a great midday feast each year on August 1 (or between July 31 and August 3). It is at this time that Lugh's shining son, Cuchulain, and his beautiful wife, Emer, can also be remembered, for their eternal love brings harmony to the Earth.

As an archetype, Emer is the embodiment of beauty. When we look for her, we are seeking what is beautiful within our own nature. Beauty can be recognized in the eternal world, but beauty as a quality of the soul has to do with the balance, harmony, perfection and integration of our True Nature. Cuchulain is the classic hero. He is the part of us that is victorious and will succeed against all odds.

Emer & Cuchulain in Nature
Songbirds, Ivy & The Clover of the Field

Emer loves the Three-Leafed Clover, which reminds us of the triple Goddess. Remember her when you walk through valleys, meadows and fields. In Judeo-Christianity the Four-Leafed Clover was said to have been brought by Eve from Paradise and is therefore considered a symbol of luck and good fortune. White Clover Flower Essence is used to help a person let go of control and accept their destiny.

Cuchulain's familiar is a Hound. So if a white dog visits you in a dream or meditation, ask yourself if Cuchulain is sending you a message. Also, every time you hear a chorus of Songbirds or see Irish Ivy climbing up a fence or wall, know that Emer and Cuchulain are celebrating in the Otherworld.

Emer's Colors
Gold, Emerald Green & Coral

Emer's three sacred colors are Gold, Emerald Green and Coral, and when combined, they become the radiant Path of Love and Beauty. Gold is the color of wealth, self-value and worthiness, which makes a Goddess radiate both wisdom and beauty. Wedding rings are made of a golden circle, which symbolizes eternal love. The Holy Grail is also sometimes seen as gold. Emer steps into marriage with the Hero Cuchulain knowing they would love fully for the time they are given. In valuing herself, she is able to treasure another.

Emerald Green opens our hearts so that we can enter into right relationships with all beings. The Goddess who radiates Emerald Green light has faith in love and relating. She lives in balance with nature, and is a master of following the wisdom of the heart.

Coral is the color of illuminated consciousness. It is the quality of a Goddess who can surrender her need for individuality in order to become part of a greater whole. Emer radiates Coral Light as part of her ability to find strength in vulnerability. Coral shines in souls who have embraced the wisdom of love and beauty. As is often true in the case of twin flames, Emer's colors are very similar to Cuchulain's.

Cuchulain's Colors
Gold, Red & Emerald Green

The three colors sacred to Cuchulain are Gold, Red and Emerald Green, and this combination is known as "The Hero." Gold is the color of splendor, wisdom and connection to the Divine. Cuchulain, the son of the Sun God Lugh, naturally radiates Golden Light.

Red is the essence of strength needed for the successful Hero. Emerald Green is the color of an open heart and also right relationship with the natural world; it can open the door to the world of the Faery-folk.

Meeting the Goddess Emer

Beauty can be observed in the physical features of others, but the quality of beauty is found within. It has little to do with the bodily appearance of another, but is instead more closely related to the Inner Light and Goodness that shines through a person.

As Emer knows, each person has a beautiful and often complex destiny that has been designed by the spiritual world especially for them. Since we have free will, the path must also be chosen. Mystics know that they are living into their life purpose and mission when they have located and are pursuing their Golden Thread. When you are ready to embrace your beauty and talents, then it is time to meet Emer.

When following our Golden Thread, we become attuned with our highest destiny, and life becomes filled with love, mystery and magic. Emer understands how to locate and weave the threads of our destiny into the fabric of our being. She is not concerned with the length of our threads, because we have each been allotted a different but perfect time on Earth. She is more interested in how well we know and live the fabric of our own design.

Practice
Following Your Golden Thread

The original spark of Light that came into being at your conception is called the Incarnational Star. It is located two finger widths below your navel and two finger widths inside. This spiritual star is the melodious part of you that moves from lifetime to lifetime without changing. Inside your Incarnational Star is a Golden Thread that will reveal your life purpose and mission.

Ask your Higher Self to reveal your Golden Thread. Then, with your inner vision, see your thread as it extends from your belly center down to the ground. If you try placing your feet on your thread, it will feel sticky, and you might have the comforting sensation of feeling at home in your body. Next, witness as your Golden Thread flies before you, shimmering like a Golden Songbird. If you touch it, you might feel as though you are suddenly riding a flying Goose. Generally, when you follow your Golden Thread, life unfolds with effortless grace and ease.

When you have an important decision to make, it is wise to invoke your Golden Thread. Remember that when you truly follow your Golden Thread, no harm can come to you. Call upon Emer's Songbirds to weave your life in the right direction. When you walk the Path of Your Highest Destiny, a bubble of protection and grace surrounds you. Like Cuchulain riding to victory, you can follow your Golden Thread through any situation—no matter how friendly or challenging.

Don't forget that there will be times when the Golden Thread will simply coil into a nest at your feet. That is a time for standing still and waiting for the cosmic eggs to hatch. You will be prompted by inner forces to move at the proper time.

Remember to treasure the Path of Your Highest Destiny. Like Emer, know that life is sacred. Commit to walking the shining thread to complete your life lessons, and live into the life purpose for which you were born. If you listen carefully, you may begin to hear the melody of the Golden Songbirds in the landscape in and around you even now...

Visualization
A Banquet with Emer & Cuchulain

Imagine that you are walking in emerald green grass. The air seems especially pure, and you have the feeling that soon something extraordinary is about to happen.

A huge golden bird circles above you. The magical bird spirals down and lands before you. It holds a sprig of Irish ivy in its beak, as a symbol that Emer and Cuchulain have invited you into their kingdom. After climbing aboard the broad back of the exquisite Golden Songbird, you are lifted up into the air. You watch as the landscape below you becomes smaller and smaller, until soon you are flying amongst the clouds. For a few moments, simply enjoy what it is like to fly through time and space.

Eventually the bird begins to spiral downwards in a counterclockwise fashion. You lean to the left, which helps you to stay balanced. As the circles become smaller and more focused, you see a fortress below you. It has stonewalls covered in Irish ivy, and gardens filled with pink roses. The Songbird lands gently, and you gracefully slip off its feathered back, thanking it for the ride. The bird places the sprig of ivy into your left hand, then flies off into the expanse of blue sky.

You look around at the stone fortress and notice a doorway which is open. Entering the fortress, you are met by a large white hound that looks ferocious. From the promptings of a silent voice, you show it the ivy, and the dog wags its shaggy tail and trots off down a corridor. Not knowing what else to do, you follow the hound. The fortress is lined with mirrors, and as you walk, you notice that you are becoming more radiant and beautiful. Your clothes also transform to match your regal surroundings.

Eventually you enter a large banquet hall. There are many nobles sitting at a long rectangular table. When you enter the hall, there is fanfare. A woman wearing a crown of gold, silver and ivy walks toward you. You realize that she is Emer, and bow to honor her great presence. A man follows her, and he is wearing a similar Otherworldly crown. He carries a shield with an emblem of a sun that shines so brightly you have to look away.

"Come and join us," says Emer. "We've been expecting you."

There is a seat between Emer and Cuchulain that is empty, and so you join them at the grand table. As you observe their finely clothed friends, you also notice some familiar faces. Sitting to your right are King Conchobar Mac Nessa who is busy eating and Cathbad the Druid who nods to welcome you. To your left, you see Manannan Mac Lir and his pale wife, Fand. At the end of the table is the shadowy Goddess Scatach, who is seated with her son, Connal who wears a headband with eagle feathers. There are also others who you have yet to meet, and they smile and raise their glasses in your honor.

"We are pleased to have the Grail initiate amongst us!" says Cuchulain. "We will ride out in battle first thing in the morning."

Not certain that you really had wished to battle amongst famous heroes, you still raise your silver cup and smile. A Grail Quest would lead you to all sorts of places you would never expect.

After you have finished a sumptuous feast, Emer leads you to the place where you will rest for the night. The stone room is warm, heated by the fireplace across from the foot of your bed. Emer smiles and then closes the door.

In the morning, Cuchulain strides in and tosses you a barbed spear. It glows in your hand, and you realize that he has given you the *Gae Bulga*, which inflicts wounds from which no one may recover. You look carefully at the spear and then back at Cuchulain.

Emer enters with her songbirds and a servant carrying a large object covered by a tapestry. You stand up, with spear in hand, and turn to face her as the servant places the object on the ground and departs. The songbirds remove the tapestry, and you discover that you are looking at yourself in a large mirror.

"Who do you see?" asks Emer.

When you look into the mirror, at first you see yourself as you are now, and then the image begins to change. You see yourself the last time you were enraged. Then the mirror shows you another time of anger, and then a third.

"You're seeing me at my worst," you say.

"Anger is a distortion of the essence of strength, which warriors need for the Quest," Cuchulain tells you.

You again look at your face in the mirror, and see it contorted in rage. This makes you feel ashamed.

"To find what is true, you must throw the *Gae Bulga*," says Cuchulain. "Into the illusion of the false self."

"What is true can never be destroyed," Emer explains.

They both look at you and smile with such sunny radiance that you sense their words and intentions are true. Drawing back the spear, you take aim at the mirror and throw.

There is a loud pop and then the sound of shattering. But it is not the glass that breaks, for the magical spear has penetrated through to another world. For a moment, you no longer know who you are. You stagger backwards, and then fall…

You fall through time and space, and as you fall, your clothes, and skin, and bones all burn up. You have become a ball of Light, one radiant sun. All that is untrue in you burns away, until what is left is the design of your True Nature.

The Golden Songbird swoops below you, and then you find that you are flying clockwise, up and up, with greater and greater strength. Soon you are amongst the clouds, and looking down, you see the emerald green grass where your journey began.

The Golden Songbird lands gently, and you slide off its back. It turns and offers you a bunch of three-leafed clover with a sprig of Irish ivy. You accept it into your left hand, your receiving hand. You stand for a moment acknowledging the gift from Emer and Cuchulain—the true, beautiful and radiant Self. The Songbird takes flight, and you watch as it flies toward the sun and disappears.

Take some time to discover who you are now that you have been unbound from the false self. Thank Emer and Cuchulain for their great gift of liberation, strength and beauty. The *Gae Bulga* has destroyed what was no longer true, and it has set you free to discover the fullness of your design. Who is this wild and free Self?

Emer's Beauty Blessing

As the first rays of morning thread golden light

Across the green ridges of mountains

The songbirds cry out to remind us

Of the Gods and Goddesses of ancient days.

They join together in a great chorus to shout

We have the strength to live this day too

And pass the initiations of both matter and spirit.

Look inside, they sing, and find what it takes

To become a hero or heroine.

The songbirds have so much to say:

When the spears of life strike your heart

Go with the lessons and know each moment

Holds luminosity, wisdom and insight.

Notice that enemies fade like shadows at dusk,

What remains, is light, eternal and beautiful.

CAER
IBORMEITH

The Myth of Caer Ibormeith

Goddess of Swans

aer Ibormeith is an Irish Goddess or Faery who had an unusual destiny. She would become a swan for a year during the October harvest festival of Samhain that marked the end of the Celtic year.. Then, the following year, she would take on the form of a princess once again. Caer Ibormeith went through these changes over and over. *Geiss* in Old Irish means swan, and in literature a poet can also be referred to as a swan. Although swans are mute, they are connected to sound and melody. As they glide through still water, it may be that they are attuned to the music of the soul that we are usually only capable of hearing when we depart this world. Perhaps if we heard this music too early, we would not be able to withstand the challenges inherent in the earthy dimension of existence.

Caer was the beautiful daughter of Prince Ethal Anbuail, one of the tall beautiful Sidhe of Sid Uamuin in Connacht. Over time, the Sidhe became thought of as Elves or Faerie-folk, and they withdrew from this world to a parallel one. Many of the Sidhe women went to Tir Na Ban, and occasionally they would peer through the veils, especially when they heard a poet speak, a musician play, or noticed a handsome young warrior. Although generally closed to mortals, there are portals to the Otherworld that can be found in forests, under stones, and even beneath the sea. Those who discover an Otherworld find it so beautiful and alluring that it is hard to stay on surface Earth.

Caer Ibormeith was able to peer between the veils of the unseen world of Tir Na Ban into the emerald green fields of Ireland. When she saw the poet Aengus for the first time, he was playing his harp at Bru na Boinne. This site, at a bend in the Boyne River, is near the Megalithic Passage tombs, Newgrange, Dowth and Knowth, which are thought to be more ancient than Stonehenge and the Egyptian pyramids. Located about 20 miles northwest of modern-day Dublin, Newgrange was known to be a portal for the Sidhe. In folklore, it is said that on certain days of the year, just when the sunlight flickered on the back of the chamber of Newgrange at dawn on the Winter Solstice, you could step between the worlds. It was in this part of Ireland, at Bru na Boinne, on a cold and blustery December day, that Caer Ibormeith fell in love with the handsome Aengus.

Words when spoken create destinies and paths. When we speak loving words to ourselves and each other the results are magical. It was during a year when Caer Ibormeith had been changed into a swan, that Aengus selected her from a flock containing 150 other swans. The number of birds is no accident. The 150 Psalms of King David, when read or spoken aloud, can provide shelter in this world. Caer was protected until she could fulfill her true destiny and discover true love.

Due to his deep and everlasting love for her, Aengus also became a swan. The pair still reside at an Otherworldly fortress near the River

Boyne. At times, they can be heard singing beautiful music, and if someone is lulled into its spell, the songs can make a listener sleep for three days and three nights and awaken knowing a bliss beyond this world.

The Myth of
Aengus Og
Irish God of Love, Beauty & Poetry

engus Og, loved by women, was always accompanied by four swans or songbirds that flew above him, symbolizing kisses. In Irish folklore, it is said that anyone who heard the songs of the poet's birds would fall in love, and for that reason, Aengus is known as the God of Love, Beauty and Poetry.

This handsome youth had an unusual beginning. When the Dagda, God of Goodness, Abundance and Fertility, met Boann, the Irish Goddess of Wisdom and white cows, they fell in love. Desiring time alone, the Dagda sent Boann's husband Elcmar away for nine months. In order to hide the affair, the God made the sun stand still until Boann gave birth to their son. Aengus (known as Oengus in Old Irish) was the result of their union.

Aengus grew up in the Boyne River Valley, and he had a particular love for the magical site known as Bru na Boinne. There the veils between the human and Faery realms are thin. Discovering that he would inherit nothing from the Dagda, Aengus asked if he could spend a day and a night at Bru na Boinne. When his father agreed, the youth said that all days and nights are the same and claimed the site as his own.

As the legend goes, Aengus dreams repeatedly about a mysterious and beautiful woman that he continues to look for upon waking. He grew so lovesick that eventually he set out wandering the Earth looking for her. Along a bend in the River Boyne (known by some as the Dragon's Mouth), Aengus recognized Caer Ibormeith in the form of a swan gliding along the water with 150 other swans. The romantic myth is celebrated in W.B. Yeats' poem, "The Song of Wandering Aengus."

Caer's Beloved
Ireland's Missing Tale

lthough she loved most lakes and streams, Caer Ibormeith particularly enjoyed sauntering along the River Boyne. There was a particular rhythm that soothed her in the way the water flowed around the glistening stones. She loved helping the yarrow, dandelions and red valerian flowers grow, because they are such wonderful herbs for healing; and also the morning glory vines so loved by the Faery-folk, because they remind us to awaken in the morning with fresh enthusiasm for life.

On warm days, children would come to pick the flowers along the river. Occasionally she would assist them with their selections, but they never noticed her. Caer wondered why, and when she asked them, the children seemed not to hear her. It was only at night when people were dreaming that Caer felt she could truly communicate with them.

As the morning glories began to shut their flowers for the evening, Caer would go to see the last rays of the setting sun reflected in the river. It seemed as though the colors sang to her, and sometimes she would sing back to them. Creation loved her, for the wind had breathed her into being.

At night, she often heard and enjoyed the music of the sylphs—the air spirits—coming from high up amongst the stars that twinkled on and off. Caer could feel her web of Light that was woven amongst the stars, and she could sense how the planets' movements and melodies orchestrated her activities. It was almost as if she were a puppet responding to singing lights. She didn't really mind because it had always been this way, or at least for as long as she could remember.

As the days went by, she walked beside the River Boyne as though searching for something that she had lost. When there were rocky places where the wind swirled, Caer discovered that she could rise up as weightless as a bird. Often Caer imagined that she was a white swan climbing the currents with the mists, and then she would rise up. She didn't want anyone to watch her because she feared they might think of this as odd.

Caer of the auburn hair also dreamt almost every night that there was a man staring at her. Becoming curious about him, Caer sometimes sang songs from the Faery realm to the man. She wondered if he could hear her. One night, Caer had been walking and secretly flying for hundreds of miles but could no longer remember why. Returning to the River Boyne, she sat by the stream in the darkness and decided to wait for an answer.

All night she sat by the river listening to the melody of the flowing currents. The problem was that Caer couldn't quite remember where she had come from. She partly recalled children playing with her by a lake and a friendly man. She could remember something of his kind face, and it seemed that once he had held her hand. But the memory escaped her as quickly as it had come.

So she sat on the river bank and decided to sing the blue song her mother had taught her, inviting the starlight to caress the pulsing water as it moved between the cold stones. A white owl landed nearby. Without prompting, but perhaps in response to her song, the owl began to hoot. The sound attracted some chirping bats, who were curious about the strange ways the hoots were bouncing off the glistening threads Caer Ibormeith was now weaving as she sang. All night long, she moved her fingers until the silver threads became interwoven with the first rays of golden sunlight.

Caer enjoyed interlacing sunlight and starlight. Out as far as the Irish Sea, the whales began to respond to her creations of Light with low sounds that moved with the current. The dolphins also decided to join the play, and some even jumped freely in the waves that crested near the rocky edge. All day, birds and insects gathered around her. Flowers began to bloom in response, and dormant seeds even began to stir within the soil. Colors from the hot core of the Earth began to make their way to the surface in the form of blossoms and rainbows. Springs began to flow in response to the music, and the roots of trees grew downward into the depths of the rich mud. All of life flourished.

Meanwhile, night after night for an entire year, Aengus had been dreaming of a woman with long auburn hair, who sang as sweetly as a lark. After awakening, he would be so distracted by her beauty that he could hardly eat or perform any normal task. Instead, Aengus wrote poetry, wishing he could read it to the young woman. At night when the stars were out, it seemed as though she could peer at him between veils. Yet during the day, he felt shut away from her. The distance between them made him grow heartsick.

One day Aengus saw a wild boar hiding behind an Ash tree. Knowing that boars know how to walk into the Otherworlds, Aengus followed the beast. He walked, then ran, trying the keep the wild boar in his sight. Eventually he was lost in a forest. He gazed up at the leaves, called out to the sunlight, and pleaded to the spirits of the forest to help him. Perhaps he was so love sick that he lost his mind in the silence of the forest.

With only her face in his mind, Aengus continued to roam in the forest hoping to find the woman of his dreams. As summer gave way to autumn, he could feel the chill settling on his skin and knew it was time to began gathering firewood to keep himself warm throughout the long winter months.

One day as Caer explored a part of the river that ran through the forest, she noticed a man with an ax. He was cutting an Ash tree, which was beginning to cry and groan. The man did not seem to care about how the tree felt.

"Excuse me," Caer said to the man. "You're killing my tree. I planted her here a hundred years ago, and she is not ready to change form yet. It isn't her time. Can't you hear that she is crying?"

The man continued to saw and hack at the tree. Caer yelled some more at the man, but he did not seem to hear her. She decided to make a bold move and walked right up to him. With all of her force, Caer knocked the ax out of his hands. The man looked startled. For a moment he looked directly at her, and then he blinked as if not believing what he was seeing. Then the man turned and fled without looking back.

Although she was angry, Caer wondered why the man feared her. She put her hands on the bleeding trunk, and soon the life force was flowing freely in the tree again. She invited the morning glories to wrap themselves around the trunk of the tree to hide the scars and help the arbor heal.

Caer sang with the stars all night as she waded in the shadowy water at the river's edge. In the morning, she saw a sight that puzzled her. The man who had been so frightened of her was sitting on a rock by the river, weeping, with his head in his hands. Gently she made her way towards him. He was young and handsome with fair hair that flowed in waves down his muscular back. As she reached out to him, Caer noticed that her own arm and hand seemed more pale and translucent than ever. When she tried to touch the man, her hand passed through him. He looked up for a moment as if startled by a breeze, and then placed his head in his hands once more.

Having never felt sadness before, Caer was puzzled by her feeling. She was much more familiar with assisting the elements and helping plants grow. The energy around the man seemed as heavy as the fog that lingered during the winter months. An idea came to her. Since he could not see her, Caer wondered if he might be able to hear her. She blew a silver strand of Light into his left ear. He responded by lifting his head and looking around. The man did not see her, but he stopped weeping. So the next time she breathed the yellow sound that makes the buttercups blossom. She watched as the man lifted his face towards the sun. His sky blue eyes welled up with tears, but this time they were tears of joy. He hummed in response. It was a crude sound, more like the gurgle of a baby, but it was so sweet that it made Caer laugh. The man laughed in response.

"What's your name?" she murmured almost silently.

"Aengus," he whispered to the air.

"You are beautiful, Aengus," she said.

"The world is beautiful," he replied, blinking in the shimmering sunlight. Her words had a healing effect on Aengus. He looked at the stones, the glistening water, and the flowers that were near him and sighed. It had seemed that the world had lost its voice and poetry, but it was starting to come back to him. It was as if he were seeing—truly seeing—for the first time. When the woman spoke, the colors around him seemed more vibrant, and the songs of the birds seemed sweeter than ever before. Aengus paused for a moment, listening to the sounds around him. He felt in love with the entire world.

"You're meant to be an artist and a poet who inspires others," said Caer, observing Aengus closely. "Your mission is to create with life."

Aengus smiled and listened to her voice, which was as gentle as the wind blowing through a garden of wildflowers.

There are moments when, for some unknown reason, the veil that separates the worlds fades, and suddenly Caer was standing in front of Aengus. He gasped, for she was the luminous woman he had seen in his dreams and longed to know. The wind caught wisps of some of her auburn hair, brushing it against his cheeks. Aengus reached toward her, and for a moment she was no longer an apparition but a living breathing woman. She handed him a silver branch with bells and he laid it on the ground. Then he took her into his arms and held her gently. She shimmered in the earthly light. Perhaps the gods were jealous, but the veils between the worlds drew together again and they could only speak in whispers.

"There's something we must do together," said Caer. "Can you hear me?"

"Yes," Aengus replied, "I know you are real because the silver branch is still with me."

"The reflection of the Otherworld can be found nature," said Caer. "We can always speak amongst the reeds by the river."

"I want to be with you," he said almost desperately.

"We will be together, but there are things we must do first."

"Anything," he whispered.

"We need to plant seeds and help all things grow—all over this Earth. Let's start here," said Caer, shaking a winged fruit off a nearby Ash tree.

The winged fruit fluttered to his feet and Aengus picked it up carefully. While holding the fruit gently in his hands, Aengus realized that he was holding the potential of a great tree. He thought about the girl, and his heart filled with such love that he felt the urge to work with the flow of all life. Taking a stick, he drew the earth back just enough to set the winged fruit, and then he covered the hole completely with dirt and leaves. Helping in this way made Aengus feel joyous. With a smile on his lips, he gathered other fruits and seeds and slipped them into his pockets, remembering to thank the trees for their gifts.

A flock of wild swans circled above them, the white tips of their wings illuminated by the light of the setting sun. Caer and Aengus watched as the last rays dipped below the horizon, and in their own way they kissed, as the Milky Way formed and the moon began her journey across the sky. It wasn't really a kiss because their lips never met, yet they had shared something special, and a deep love was exchanged.

In the morning, Aengus watched the sunrise. He pulled the rays of Light into his heart, charging his body with energy to help with the newly assigned task of planting fruits and seeds. It was clear that this was his life purpose, because it gave him such deep bliss. Over the years as he worked, poems came to him, which he remembered and shared with others. People told him the poems were a great inspiration to them, for they offered hope and sustained life.

Aengus never knew it, but from that time by the river onward Caer followed him during all the days he spent on Earth. Every time he planted a tree or a bulb of a flower, she bent and kissed it, activating the life force within. Many other people noticed that Aengus was very happy, so they also decided to plant trees and flowers. Without even realizing it, people all over the world cooperated with life and healed the environment so that the stars and sunlight could marry once again. With love, all things thrive.

On the day Aengus left his body, he had been writing poetry by the River Boyne. He had taken a seat on the grassy shore and watched as 150 swans landed in the deep blue water. It seemed to him that feathers began to sprout from his fingertips, then along his arms, and soon he was covered in silver and white feathers. Caer was waiting for him amongst the swans, and she also sprouted wings and flew to accompany him.

"I have saved the best of my poetry for this moment with you," exclaimed Aengus. But when he spoke, it was the melody of the stars that came through his lips.

When Caer and Aengus touched, their love was so deep that the Light of their bodies fused into one radiance, like a single diamond. Sometimes, on a very clear night, if you look to the east just above the horizon, you might see a star that pulses with all the colors of the rainbow. That is Caer and Aengus, now known as the Caring Light that touches all who wish to remember. If you take in a deep breath and then hum out a tone, you might find that the love that fills all of creation may wish for you to plant seeds also. Listen closely and perhaps you too will hear Caer and Aengus singing to you. If you do, please write down the words and then dance in celebration, for you are also a dream of sound and light.

Healing with
Caer & Aengus

Finding Caer & Aengus
Love & The Celtic New Year

As archetypes Caer and Aengus are the embodiments of unconditional love. The love we have for one another can be celebrated at any time, but particularly each turning of the seasonal wheel. Each year on June 9, people wear red and go out beside the Boyne River (or any body of water) to celebrate the beloved union of Caer and Aengus. It is an auspicious day to call love into your life.

The Divine pair is also celebrated on the Celtic New Year, between October 31 and November 2 during Samhain, when the veils between surface Earth and the Otherworlds are thin. Between the Winter Solstice and Christmas Eve, Caer and Aengus can be honored by decorating the home with twigs from a silver tree, or the slender branches of an Ash. Love is always celebrated on May 1 during Beltane. It is also on these days that swans can act as guides to help us move between dimensions.

Caer in Nature
Ash & Swans

Caer did not want Aengus to cut down the Ash tree (which drops winged fruit), because it is one of a trilogy of trees sacred to the Druids. In Irish folklore, it is said that the Tuatha Dé brought the Ash tree (*Nin* in Old Irish) from Tir Na n-og. In Norse mythology, the Ash is known as the *Yggdrasil* or World Tree that connects the nine worlds in that cosmology. Poets say that the essence of the Ash tree helps people stand in their truth, and it is through the Ash tree that Caer and Aengus first met. The Ash is Caer's sacred tree.

The Swan is a symbol of our eternal essence. In ancient Ireland, bards would sometimes wear a cloak made of feathers, including swan feathers, known as a *tuigen*. Sacred to the Druids, swans represented the soul's ability to move with ease between worlds. In myth and legend, swans are often known as shape-shifters. When you see a pair of swans, remember that love is eternal and the Otherworld is close.

Aengus in Nature
Reeds & A Wild Boar

In folklore, it is said that doorways to the Blessed Isle can sometimes be found amongst the Reeds where Swans gather. The medicine of the Common Reed is a powerful one. It reminds us that if we bend down low during a storm, then we can survive and rise again another day.

Aengus's familiar is the fearless Boar or Wild Pig. Boars have sharp tusks and are greatly feared, but are generally shy and avoid humans. Bards would sometimes tell stories of those who had received the gift of prophecy running with or shape-shifting into a wild boar. Druids associated the boar with spiritual authority.

Caer's Colors
Silvery Blue, Rose Pink & Orange

Caer's sacred colors are Silvery Blue, Rose Pink and Orange, like the colors of the sunrise. A Goddess who radiates Silvery Blue never loses her connection with the Otherworlds, but can slip like a magical swan between time, space and dimension.

Rose Pink is the color of feminine intuition and the ability to listen to another so they feel loved unconditionally. The color pink also helps us hear the whispers of faeries and elementals, encouraging us to help the planet thrive. Orange connects us to pleasure, creativity and the art of love. The color orange helps us heal after a shock or betrayal, allowing us to settle and live out our life purpose and mission.

Together this combination of blue, pink and orange is known as the "Caring Light." Caer reminds us that even when we live on the other side of the world, or even in another dimension, it is still possible to love another deeply.

Aengus' Colors
Gold, Light Blue & Red

Gold, Light Blue and Red are the three colors sacred to Aengus. This is the combination of musicians, wise bards, poets and others who help us anchor the Light on Earth. Gold is the color of Wisdom and the thread that leads the Hero on the journey of his highest evolutionary path. Light Blue offers the Hero a direct link with the Divine, so he can communicate to those in the Otherworlds. Red is the color of Strength and Discipline, soul qualities we need to succeed on our Quest.

Meeting the Faery-Goddess Caer

Caer can remind your Higher Self how to peer through the veils and discover sweetness. Her gift for you is Love, and she understands much about the magical arts of intimacy. Of course, to find love in the external world, we must feel and embody an extraordinary amount of Self-Love. We need to have unwrapped the gift of love and understand that the source is found within our own hearts.

When you are ready to awaken to the next level of love in your life, call upon Caer. Take a moment to place your hand on your heart and feel the wellspring of loving kindness that flows from your soul to you always. When you are feeling happy and fulfilled, it is time to seek a relationship, because who you find yourself in relationship with is always a reflection of yourself. If you enjoy the sweet magic of Faery-folk, then try the next exercise to help yourself understand more about the essence of Love.

Practice
A Faery's Wreath of Love

You will need:
A White Plate or Dish
6 Red Candles with Holders
6 Pieces of Rose Quartz
Flower Petals
1 Dark-Colored Bowl
Rose, Jasmine or Lotus Essential Oil
Pure Spring Water

Do this practice when you are ready to understand more about the essence of Love. Around a white plate or dish, place six red candles in the shape of a heart. As you light the candles, ask for Caer's assistance and invoke the quality of Love in your life. Take six pieces of rose quartz and place them in a heart shape outside of the candle heart. Then take high frequency flower petals, such as from roses, and sprinkle them outside of the rose quartz forming a third heart, three being a number sacred to the Goddess.

Take a dark-colored small bowl (black or indigo works best) and fill it with pure water. Next, carefully place the bowl beneath the wreath of love that you have created.

Now close your eyes and become perfectly still. Put your hands on the bowl of water and ask your Higher Self to send you a feeling of Love. Be aware of the sensations in your body. If you would like to have a relationship or strengthen the sweetness of the relationship you are in, simply imagine being in love. Water can act as a threshold or portal to another world. Ask that Caer be present with you. Opening your eyes, peer into the water and ask the Goddess to help you catch a glimpse of your beloved and the life you will have together.

Only good can happen when we are in a state of Love and call for an even greater understanding of it. You can take the exercise further by writing in your journal, or drawing, or making a collage of the images that you have seen. Then when you're ready, blow out the candles, and thank your Higher Self for helping you to see into the Otherworlds.

Visualization
The Bells of Faery-Folk

Imagine that you have entered a sacred forest. You are drawn to a large Ash tree, which must be hundreds of years old. Notice that your vision shifts and, with open or closed eyes, you can see into the world of the Sidhe. A slender female steps out of the trunk of the tree. From the feathers in her hair, you know the Swan Faery-Goddess Caer has decided to visit you. Smiling, Caer Ibormeith invites you to follow her through a portal into the Otherworld. She shape-shifts into a swan, and soon you realize that you're also sprouting feathers, and then wings. Together you fly along a river. It feels good to be light and free.

Notice that there is a bend in the wide river. The water seems to shimmer as you fly down closer to it, and you land in the water wondrously, with grace and ease. Once you walk out of the water, your white swan feathers drop away, and a youthful and healthy version of your eternal self is revealed. With great reverence, you peer down into the dark water from the riverbank.

Keep your mind open and simply keep gazing into the darkness of the water. Allow your imagination to be free so that it can play. Be receptive and simply receive whatever images and sensations come to you. Then when you feel complete, thank Caer and the Great Goddess. Close your eyes and be with the sweetness of the moment.

Another swan lands on the river, and you realize that Aengus Og has joined you. Your body becomes enchanted once again, and soon you again sprout feathers and the wings of a swan. Then you begin flying with both Caer and Aengus. The love they have for one another is so potent that you are filled with bliss. Flying past the tree with silver and golden apples, you hear the bells of the Faery-folk, and know you are being blessed.

As the sun begins to set, all three of you fly into the Light. Magically, you discover that you have re-entered surface Earth. You see the great Mother Ash tree and you spiral back down to your body—whole, happy and complete. Notice that you're holding a small silver branch with a golden apple. Caer and Aengus Og are smiling upon you.

Caer's Blessing

This blessing is for all the people of the world.

May we awaken together,

May we remember who we are,

Why we are here

And how to live together.

May we be sensitive to the needs of the Earth

And the vulnerability of the living oceans.

May we remember how to attune

To all sentient beings,

For the world is alive.

May we remember that together

We create solutions

That bring solace to the world.

May we remember that together

We are fulfilled.

CAILLEACH

Quest for Earth's Cauldrons

There are henges, cairns, caves and passage tombs on the surface of the earth that act as entrances or portals to Otherworlds. They are often located near water, but some are found on mountains. Newgrange is an excellent example of a passage tomb in Ireland, and there is still some debate as to whether it is a burial site, an ancient healing temple, or a doorway to the Sidhe. There are other landscapes known for Otherworld activity, such as Fairy's Wood in Sligo, Ireland, and the Fairy Hill of Caledonia in Scotland. In fact, there are thin places all over the world. Where you discover a myth in the landscape, you will probably also find an ancient truth. Those of the unseen worlds live amongst the seen. In this last legend, the Goddess Brighid goes in search of the Crone Goddess known as the Cailleach, perhaps the greatest shape-shifter of all time.

Cailleach in her maiden form.

The Cailleach in Myth & Legend
A Self-Created Goddess

The Cailleach (pronounced "KAL-y-ach" or "coyluck") is one of the world's greatest and most ancient Goddesses, predating the Celts by seven thousand years. She has many names including Cailleach Bheur, Scota or Carlin in Scotland; The Hag of Beare or Digne in Ireland; Black Annis in Britain; and Cailleach ny Groamch on the Isle of Man. She is sometimes depicted as a giantess with a blue-black face and one eye, who leaps from mountaintop to mountaintop, dropping boulders from her apron to create hills. Cailleach becomes furious with those who disrespect Nature and causes storms to rage during her tempests.

The Cailleach is sovereign and self-created. She has no parents, yet is married to all humankind. Men are sacred to her, yet she has no children—although in folklore, she fostered 50 or more. She can be a beautiful young maiden, or the ugly hag of winter whose hair is matted in frost. The Cailleach is the Goddess who stands between life and death. Her single eye sees beyond duality. She embraces the Oneness of all existence.

The word Hag arises out of the Greek word for holywoman or wisewoman. A deep Ancestress who understands the passage of time, Cailleach often appears as an old woman, but has the ability to perpetually renew her youth. In many of the Celtic stories, the hag, when kissed, becomes a young and beautiful maiden. This Goddess is full of surprises, and you never quite know how she might show up. Animals are dear to her, including bears, deer, cats and crows. As ancient as she is, the wild places call to her heart. In Celtic mythology, kings married the land in order to rule. Cailleach is the ancient earth, the lichen-covered rocks, mountain peaks, frost and snow-covered fields.

Cailleach is sometimes called Grandmother, Keeper of Wisdom, the Blue-Faced Hag, or the Queen of Winter. There are many tales still told in which the Callieach loved men who aged and died, while she lived on into the next spring, and would find yet another pretty, young man to share her bed. Stories of Kundry, Ragnall and other Loathy Ladies are those of the thinly disguised Goddess, the Cailleach.

Brighid in Myth & Legend
Goddess of Poetry & Healing

One of the most contradictory yet enduring Goddesses, Brighid has moved easily through the centuries. In Irish mythology, Brighid means "the exalted one." She has been worshipped for over fifteen hundred years and is known as the "Holy Fire." As a Goddess, she is the daughter of the Dagda (the God of Goodness, Abundance and Fertility) and Boann (the Irish Goddess of Poetry and of the River Boyne). Brighid is known for her poetic and healing talents, as well as her more practical knowledge of smithcraft. She was originally worshipped as a Triple Goddess.

There was an all-female priesthood of Brigid in Kildare, where women trained in healing and in the ancient ways of the Goddess. The priesthood had laws that protected women from rape, and trained women interested in warrior skills for battle. Many of her priestesses became guardians of holy springs, wells, groves and caves.

A complex figure, Brigit (with several spellings of her original name Brighid) is also recognized as one of the most powerful of all

Christian saints. Saint Brigit, who died in 525 AD, absorbed much of the power of the magical early Goddess. A flame was kept burning in her honor until King Henry VIII had it extinguished during the reformation.

The Seer-poets have kept her oral poetic tradition alive. Her most ancient name is *Breo-saighead*, meaning "fiery arrow." Saint Brigit is sometimes referred to as *Muire na nGael* or Mary of the Gael, and is considered by many to be the great mother of the Celts. Along with Saint Patrick, Saint Brigit is considered the patron Saint of Ireland.

In the United Kingdom, Brigid is known as Brigantia, and she may be the personification of Britain. Both the wizard Merlin and the poet Taliesin describe her as a Goddess of Sovereignty concerned with justice and human potential. An ancient and well-loved Goddess, Brighid was incorporated by the Celtic Church as Brigit, the midwife or foster-mother of Jesus.

Sexuality and motherhood were considered sacred to the Celts. Brighid is known and loved as a mother who fights for the health and well-being of her children. During the feast of Imbolc, corn dolls are made in her honor. Young maidens would give the dolls to the men they wished to bed, and this aspect of Imbolc ensured the birth of new children and a continuation of life.

Irish Goddess Brighid was the sister of Aengus Og and later married the Formorian King Bres. They had one son named Ruadan, who died. Thus she also brings us the art of keening, a type of singing or wailing for those we have lost. The original Goddess was never imagined to be a virgin, but instead the consort of whatever man she chose. Brighid continues to remind us of the Eternal Light that lives within each one of us.

Brighid as the Grail Maiden

Brighid's Search for the Cailleach
Ireland & Britain's Missing Tale

The autumn leaves had begun to fall and crispness returned to the air. As fall gave way to winter, a thought occurred to Brighid one day. While she had come to know many of the Goddesses, there was one she had still not met. She felt a strong need to meet the Cailleach, the most ancient one of all.

Brighid had been told that the Cailleach could appear as a beautiful, young maiden or as a one-eyed, blue-faced old hag. Brighid decided that in order to know the keeper of the Earth's wisdom, she must meet this Goddess in person. She would decide for herself whether the Cailleach was a beautiful queen or an ugly blue-faced crone.

Brighid took her corn dolly, made in honor of the Goddess, down from her altar place. She wrapped a few sandwiches in some cloth and put on her green cloak. Then she headed out toward the northern-most mountains, where the cold winter winds blew ferociously.

It took a long time to find a path to the Cailleach. Each time Brighid asked townspeople for directions, they would point to the mountains and then quickly shut their doors.

"She must be very frightening," thought Brighid, "if people will not even mention her name."

One day, as Brighid walked north toward the mountains of the ancient ones, she saw a young child chasing a butterfly. The little child seemed so happy and carefree.

"What is your name?" Brighid asked the girl-child.

"I am Carlin," she said.

"Where are your mother and father?"

"I have no mother or father," said the child.

"How sad," said Brighid.

"Not really. I never knew them, so it was like they never lived. At least not here."

"Who looks after you?"

"I look after myself," answered the child, who then scampered up the hill and disappeared behind the blackthorn bushes.

Brighid called out to her, but the child did not take heed. Worried that Carlin might encounter danger in the frigid landscape, Brighid followed her. She shouted again to the child, who she thought she could see running playfully in and out of the shadows. Eventually Brighid had travelled so far that she realized she'd lost her way. The last rays of light were disappearing. Brighid could barely see the ancient mountains to the north.

As darkness overtook the forest, Brighid became afraid. She could see eyes staring at her. Once an animal came so close that Brighid

218

yelled, before she realized that it was only a startled deer. The doe then leapt away into the night.

"Perhaps the deer had come to help me," thought Brighid sadly.

Clouds gathered above her and it began to snow. She wished for the warmth of a hearth, some warm soup, and a bed where she could sleep. Brighid became quite worried that she might freeze to death. She also felt sorry for the child who could perish on such a cold night, but decided she must save herself. Brighid began searching for a cottage in the woods where she might rest and find safety.

Once or twice she was certain that a bear growled nearby, and the fear kept Brighid moving along the silvery paths of moonlight in the snow. In time, off in the distance, she saw the warm glow of a house. Hurrying across the frosty earth, she reached the cottage just as the full moon rose. She realized it was a hunter's cabin, for the porch was littered with furs and the bones of animals. Brighid was so cold that she knocked on the door anyway.

The fair-haired lad who answered was bare-chested, and the fire from the nearby hearth cast a radiant glow on his youthful skin. His good looks surprised her, and although Brighid would not normally have entered a man's house alone, there was little choice.

When he offered to share his bed with her, Brighid looked at the warm furs and climbed in. That night she made love with the man and never asked his name.

In the morning he was gone, but an old woman standing at the hearth was stirring a cauldron. The cottage was small, but clean and warm. There were herbs hanging from beams, and the smell of the cooked food piqued Brighid's appetite.

"My son said you were hungry, so I made you some soup," said the woman, who then smiled. Brighid noticed that the old woman had only one tooth. "You'll need it to keep the child that grows like a seed within you nourished."

Brighid blushed and asked the name of her son, and the old woman replied, "His name is Man."

"I thought he might have his own name," said Brighid.

"Some call him Beare," the woman told her, continuing to stir the pot. "But child, they are all one and the same."

When Brighid asked where the young hunter went, the old woman replied that he had gone to the ancient mountains in the north where the Cailleach lives.

Brighid was excited that someone knew the way to the Ancient Goddess. She asked the woman many questions between her sips of soup.

"Take this for your journey," offered the old woman. "It will keep you strong." She handed Brighid a loaf of seed bread, which the girl slipped into her green cloak.

The morning sun had melted most of the snow, and Brighid thanked the old woman for her hospitality before stepping outside. Then she followed her host's directions to the ancient hills where the Cailleach was said to drop boulders from her apron as she leapt from mountaintop to mountaintop. Brighid hoped she would encounter the fair hunter again somewhere on her journey.

The forest gave way to bare ground covered in stones, which gave way to boulders covered with lichen. The large rocks looked as though symbols and messages had been etched into their craggy faces. Twice Brighid looked back at them, wondering if one might indeed be the Cailleach, but the only movement was the wind. As Brighid began to climb the first mountain, she realized that she'd forgotten to ask the old woman for her name.

When the sun was at its zenith, Brighid saw crows circling and thought that perhaps her fair-haired hunter had caught something for dinner. Moving slowly so she would not slip, Brighid quietly climbed over the slick boulders and peeked out—hoping to see the hunter. Instead, she saw bears gnawing on the carcass of a deer. She shuffled backwards trying not to make a sound, wanting to avoid becoming their next dinner.

As Brighid turned around, she noticed a man watching her from between two rocks that lay together like hands in prayer. She was hoping that it would be the young hunter, but this man was dark and grizzled from many years spent in the mountains. Still he welcomed her into his bed at a cabin that night, and she made love with him to keep warm.

In the morning when Brighid awoke, the old woman was stirring a pot hanging over a fire in the fireplace. Brighid blushed, realizing that the old woman knew how she had spent the night. The old woman smiled showing her one tooth.

"You like my sons," said the old woman.

"Yes," Brighid told her, realizing it was best to be truthful.

"Here's some soup to warm you and a loaf of seed bread for your journey. You need nourishment for the child that grows within you."

Again, Brighid asked for directions, and the old woman told her to keep climbing the northern face of the mountain, and that soon she would find what she was looking for.

Brighid climbed between the moss-covered boulders all day. She had trouble catching her breath, because the air was thin; few plants grew at that altitude. It was cold, and Brighid wished she had brought gloves and a warmer coat. Brighid climbed, once again realizing that she had forgotten to ask the old woman her name. But she ate the loaf of bread and was fortified by the seeds, and continued on her way.

The sun sank quickly behind the mountains, and soon Brighid again began searching for a warm place to spend the night. As she approached the entrance of another hunter's cabin, Brighid hoped she could warm herself without taking in another man. But when the hunter opened the door, he was more handsome than the other two, and she quickly snuggled under the covers with him. He was such an excellent lover that she forgot to ask his name or where the Cailleach lived.

As the morning rays made their way through the windows of the cottage, Brighid saw the old woman with the single tooth sitting by the fire stirring a pot. Humming as she stirred, the old woman seemed content in her wrinkled skin. An orange tabby cat was lying across her lap purring.

"Most women like my third son best," she said.

This time Brighid did not blush, because the woman did not seem judgmental of her nightly dalliances.

"What's his name?" asked Brighid.

"Man," answered the old woman. "Because they are all the same."

"Who is his father?"

"No one," said the old woman, who then continued to hum.

Brighid thought that the old woman must have lived a hard life, yet she seemed free in her elder years. She felt more comfortable knowing that the old woman knew the truth about life, and what it takes to survive when winter is approaching and it is cold outside.

"I made you porridge this morning," the old woman told her. She handed Brighid a steaming bowl of oats.

"How is it," asked Brighid, "that I spend all day as a young woman climbing a summit and looking for the Cailleach, and yet you always arrive at the same place?"

"I am strong," replied the old woman, "and used to these hills."

"How many sons do you have?" asked Brighid.

"I have fifty foster sons, none from my womb, and yet all children come from me." The old woman stroked the purring cat.

As Brighid looked at the old woman, she thought it odd that frost dripped from her apron even though it was warm in the cottage.

"What's your name?"

"Some call me the Hag of Beare," said the old woman, smiling and showing her one crooked tooth that looked red in the dawning light. She was so ugly that Brighid shivered slightly.

"You have been so kind. How can I repay you?"

The old woman laughed so hard that the cat jumped down and ran away. Brighid thought her response was a little strange. Even so, she pulled out a coin purse and gave the woman a golden coin that she had been saving for the right moment. The Hag of Beare looked at the coin, bit it and then threw it into the fire. Brighid was startled by her action.

"Why did you throw the coin in the fire? It was valuable!" she exclaimed.

"You can't eat gold," said the old woman. "Not in these ancient mountains. Besides, there are plenty of seeds to keep us going until the spring rains come and the flowers cover the hillsides."

Once again the old woman handed Brighid a loaf of seed bread and told her to continue to travel north, and that soon she should find what she was looking for.

"Is the Cailleach as wise as people say she is?" asked Brighid. "And what does she look like?"

"She's as ancient as the mountains and has many faces," said the old woman. "Some say she is wise and others call her an old fool."

"Where does she live?"

"What would you expect her home to look like?" asked the Hag of Beare.

"If she's the greatest and most ancient of all the Goddesses, I imagine she would live in an enchanted realm, where her walls sparkle with frost, and her floors are made of ice, above which she hangs snowflakes in her silver chandeliers," said Brighid, hoping this might be the case.

The Hag of Beare laughed aloud again, slapping her knees and almost spilling the cauldron of porridge.

"Have you been to her house?"

"Many times," said the old woman.

"What's it like?"

"It changes in every season," replied the old woman, handing Brighid a second loaf of bread. "You'll need two loaves for the journey home, if you choose to make it," she explained.

Again the old woman gave Brighid directions.

This part of the summit was steep, but Brighid moved briskly, encouraged by the idea that today she would find the Cailleach, the most ancient Goddess of them all.

When the sun was high overhead, Brighid finally reached the mountaintop. She was puzzled because there was no house as far as one could see. She called out: "Beloved Ancient Goddess Cailleach. Please come and find me. I have looked for you for many days now and it would be a great honor to meet you."

After a few moments passed, Brighid saw the child she had met at the beginning of her journey. The girl was still chasing butterflies.

"Carlin!" she exclaimed. "Thank goodness, you're all right!"

"Why shouldn't I be?" asked the child, who walked over to Brighid and stood by her.

"Well, a snow storm came and I was afraid you might perish!" said Brighid, who suppressed the impulse to brush the child's matted hair.

Carlin giggled, and then she looked directly at Brighid and said, "I made sure you were safe. I always led you to my brothers."

Brighid was confused. "Are you the Cailleach?" she asked.

"I am a face of the ancient one," she replied. Then the child added, "I am hungry. May I have one of your seed loaves?"

"Of course," said Brighid, reaching into her cloak for the bread that had hardened in the cold air.

"But I told you this morning that you'll need two loafs for the journey home, if returning is what you now choose," said the child. "If I eat this loaf, you'll starve."

Brighid slowly returned the bread to her cloak. Then she looked closely at the child who smiled, revealing one single crooked tooth.

"So... you have been with me from the beginning," said Brighid. "You were with me from the moment I looked for you."

"I have been with you since the beginning of time and will be with you to the end," said the Cailleach.

As they spoke, it seemed that the golden rays of the sun fortified the child's hair in a way that caused it to grow. As Brighid watched, the child became a young and stunningly attractive woman.

"I am never what I first appear to be," said the Cailleach.

"I can see why young men might fall in love with you," said Brighid.

"That's really your role," said the Cailleach. They both laughed.

"What are the names of your brothers? I know one is Beare."

"They are also me," Cailleach said, with a sly grin.

They both slapped their knees and roared with laughter.

"So you truly are all things, and I might know you more intimately than I intended," said Brighid.

"For an old single-eyed blue-faced hag with one crooked tooth, I do pretty well."

"Please tell me more about yourself," said Brighid. "I've come a long way to rest on this summit with you."

The Cailleach looked off into the distance and took a long sigh, then began her tale. "I formed myself out of mountains when the days of the Earth were still young, and I am still here. There is nothing in this world that has not passed through me. I have been breathing through the soil, through the stones and through the lichen that grows on them since the very first winter. I am the frost on your windowpane, the fine lines on your cheeks, the trees after they have lost their leaves. I am with all things as they rest and change. I am the Cailleach, the Hag of Winter, the oldest and most frightening Goddess you'll ever meet. I can also come to you as a maiden in the spring, or a young man in the darkest night. I am an ugly old woman, and yet I am revered by all who find me. Eventually, every man who ever lives will kiss me, and every woman too, as your bodies return to the dark earth. I will also breathe life into you when you return, for I understand the cycles of life, death and re-birth."

For many hours, Brighid visited with the Cailleach, who stood on the peak of the mountain with sunlight and shadows pulling at her frost apron. As the sun set and shadows crossed over the mountains, the Winter Goddess's face became blue and one eye became cloudy. Stars appeared in the dark sky that seemed to hold Brighid in a cosmic womb, and she felt warm even as wind howled across the summit.

Looking into the potent darkness, Brighid said, "It's a great honor to meet you, Grandmother. I'm glad I looked for you because I no longer fear life or death."

"And why is that?" asked the Cailleach, who had become an ancient woman with long white hair who walked bent over. The Hag of Beare reached inside her frosty apron and took out a cauldron that began to glow with supernatural warmth.

"I'm happy I met you because I know you look after me, and you always will," said Brighid. "After all, you have given me new life."

"My son did that," said the Cailleach, patting Brighid's belly. "He is part of me and I am part of him."

"And what is his name?"

"Man," she answered. "He has many names and many faces. Just call him Hunter."

"Will he be with me when I birth my child?" Brighid asked.

"Perhaps yes and perhaps no," said the Cailleach. "But I will be with you and you will have a child." She put her long right index finger inside her cauldron and then licked it.

Brighid thought that the Cailleach looked luminous.

"Want to try some?" said the Cailleach, offering her the Grail.

Brighid hesitated, not knowing what tasting from the Grail might entail. "No, thank you. I'm grateful for the gift you have already given me," said Brighid laying her hands comfortably on her belly.

"Did you find everything you were looking for?" asked the Cailleach, as clouds moved across the sky and thick snowflakes began to fall.

"I believe so," said Brighid. "I followed a child up toward the mountain, I met some men and a grandmother, and realized that we are all the same. I have been given a new life and a new understanding."

The Cailleach smiled and said, "Well, good. Then come to my enchanted garden so that we may hang snowflakes together."

Brighid shivered and, looking at the old woman with the frosty apron, said, "No Grandmother, I'm not ready for your lap just yet." Brighid thought of the hunters in their cozy homes, and also the life that grew within her. "Did you say these seed loaves have enough sustenance for my journey home?" Brighid asked.

"I give you my word," said the Cailleach, who was becoming so white that she almost seemed silver.

"Then I will make my journey home," said Brighid.

As Brighid spoke, the dawning rays of morning began to spread pink light across the snow-covered earth. The young woman turned to look at the sunrise. When Brighid turned back around to say good-bye to the Cailleach, she did not see anything but a crow gliding quietly amongst the ancient peaks.

The triquetra or trinity knot symbolizes our
eternal connection with the land, sea and sky.

Healing with Brighid & the Cailleach

Finding the Goddess Cailleach
The Winter Months

The Cailleach is traditionally celebrated on January 1. As Queen of Winter, her reign begins at Samhain (October 31 or November 1) and lasts through the winter months, particularly January when the cold north wind blows. Winter is a time of honoring the seeds that sleep deep within the Earth awaiting the time of their new birth in spring. Although the surface of the Earth might be chilly, the warmth of the Earth holds the potency, creativity and possibility of life.

January is a time to dream about the year to come, to write in journals and rest by a crackling fire. The Cailleach reminds us that although we love sunlight and action, darkness and rest are equally important. Upon waking in the morning, write down your dreams. The Cailleach may be whispering secrets to you.

Celebrating Brighid
The Summer Months

Brighid, Keeper of the Sacred Flame (her sacred symbol), is celebrated on February 1 at the feast of Imbolc (pronounced "IM-bulk"). Imbolc—a Celtic festival resting between the Winter Solstice and Spring Equinox—divides winter in half.

As a Solar Goddess, Brighid is invited to hang her cloak on the sunlight and invite in the warming rays of springtime. Since flames cannot harm her, candles and fires are lit in her honor.

Falling 40 days after Christmas, Saint Brigit's Day celebrates the purification of Mary after the birth of her son Jesus. The Egyptians celebrated this day as the Feast of Nut, mother of the Sun God Ra. In Irish Gaelic tradition, a piece of clothing of each member of the family was left outside for Brighid to bless with healing energies.

The Cailleach in Nature
Blackthorn & Cat

The Cailleach is found in the wintery months, in ice, mountains and rocks. Blackthorn *(Prunus spinosa)* is thought to ward off negative energies. Because the Cailleach intimately understands the process of transformation, she is associated with the Blackthorn. When used as a flower essence, the Blackthorn flower helps when we feel overwhelmed by negative emotions, and is said to assist in transforming darkness into light.

The Cailleach's sacred animal is the Cat, that sits on your lap to keep you warm, but also keeps the house clear of rodents. She can appear too as a Deer or Bear, even a Crow. The Cailleach is the ultimate Shapeshifter, so when you call upon her she may appear as anyone or anything.

Brighid in Nature
Spring into Winter

Brighid is associated with the warming rays of the sun, which invite winter to thaw into spring. She offers the promise of summer, new life and a full harvest. All of nature loves Brighid, and her sacred animals include Lambs and milking Cows. She is a guardian of Grains and Grasses.

The Cailleach's Colors
Black, Blue & Silvery White

The triple colors of the Cailleach are similar to the robes of winter when the dark Earth sleeps under a blanket of snow. Seeds sleep in her lap awaiting the dreams of springtime. A Goddess who radiates luminous darkness can embrace us like a dark well or the nighttime sky so that we disappear. We return understanding that we are part of the Totality of all that is. When we enter the void we can attune to the Dreams of Winter, so that we can assist the process of new life. As a healing color, black represents essential power.

Goddesses that radiate Blue light can do strange and unexpected things, like the shape-shifting Cailleach who teaches us that she is all things. Blue assists us in singing or communing with the Great Goddess. Silver is the color of the threads that link us to the cosmic webs of life. White is the steadfast mountain that helps us endure.

This deeply healing color combination supports us in overcoming our dualistic or "black and white" thinking, and instead attune with the Totality of life. The Cailleach holds our dreams until they are ready to come forth, and so this color combination is called the "Dreams of Winter."

Brighid's Colors
Orange, Gold & Green

The triple colors of Brighid are related to the life-affirming rays of the sun and the plants that flourish when the Earth is in balance. This combination supports the Sacred Flame that burns within each one of us and the opening of the compassionate heart.

Orange is the color of creativity, birth and art. It is a color that helps us heal, overcome trauma and live again. Orange is also the color of sacred sexuality. Gold is the color of our innate wisdom and the intelligence that keeps us aligned with our life purpose and mission. Green is the robe of the springtime Goddess that supports the evolution and unfoldment of our True Nature and the entire Globe. It is the robe of the one who co-creates with the Sacred Flame of life.

Meeting the Goddess Cailleach

The Cailleach invites us to fully embrace where we currently are in our life cycles. We are eternal beings, and each moment is a gift. Any time we are facing a major change in our life (such as a shift in career, a move, separation, menopause, or the death of a loved one), the Cailleach can be called upon to help us remember the natural rhythms of life, death and re-birth. The Cailleach is not afraid of illness, aging or death, for she knows she is eternal.

As winter months give way to spring, the wise Cailleach can remind us that even as an old phase ends, new life will come again. And then it is the springtime Goddess, Brighid, who encourages us to drop the guise of the blue-faced Hag of Winter and become a child again.

Practice
Awareness of the Moon

Go outside at night and become aware of the phase of the moon. A new or dark moon signals a time for rest and relaxation. As the waxing crescent moon grows to a plump gibbous moon, it is a time to plant seeds and develop new ideas. The full moon is the time in which living energies are the most potent, and our ideas can easily come to fruition. As the moon wanes, we enter a period of reflection and can release what no longer serves us.

Moving into alignment with the moon helps us understand the nature of the Cailleach. Although we are often frightened of aging, the Cailleach loves us through all phases of our lives, including our triumphs, our illnesses and our defeats. The Cailleach always offers us her lap to rest upon, especially during the dark or new moon, before Brighid awakens with the promise of new life.

Visualization
Mysteries of the Cave

The beauty of the Cailleach comes from her knowledge that she is part of everything that exists in the universe. Close your eyes, and imagine that you are walking during wintertime toward a mountain covered in snow. You are wearing warm clothes and boots, but you can see the white steam your breath makes as you walk toward the highest peak. As you walk, you see crows flying above you, and notice the large boulders that adorn the landscape.

A deer approaches you. She looks thin and gaunt, and you offer her an apple from your pocket. The deer takes it from you, and when she bites it, she turns into the Queen of Winter, the Cailleach. For a moment you shiver, for she is the oldest person you have ever seen. One of her eyes is white with blindness, while the other seems as dark as the nighttime sky. She peers at you with her one seeing eye and then invites you to follow her, as she walks through a cave into the dark earth. You hesitate for a moment, asking the Divine Light to lead, guide and protect you as you learn about the mysteries of the cave.

You walk in darkness, following the sound of her footsteps. Eventually the cave opens up into a vast room that has an underground waterfall flowing through it. There is a body of still water, and the Cailleach invites you to look into its depths to see something about yourself. You notice that when you look at the reflection of the Cailleach in the water, that she appears as a radiantly beautiful maiden.

Curious about the mysteries, you bend forward and look into the water that appears shiny and black. As you look carefully, the waters

241

begin swirling, and soon they begin to reveal the mysteries of your life. As you look at the water with the Cailleach, you see the stars in the vast nighttime sky. Then you review your life from your earliest memories to the present moment. You may also review your future.

Now ask the Cailleach for something you need to see that will help you on your Grail Quest. Watch as images form, and you are shown something significant that is especially for you. When you are ready, look up and see the Cailleach smiling. Converse with her about what you have seen. Notice that she accepts you exactly as you are, completely and totally.

When you are ready to return to surface Earth, Brighid leads you back out of the cave and down the mountain to your home. As you walk, you realize the first flowers of springtime are beginning to blossom. Thank the Cailleach for sharing her secrets with you.

Song of the Cailleach

I am the rocks, the sky and air.

I am the old dead leaves of winter.

I am frozen brooks and melting ponds.

There was never a moment when I was far from you.

I loved you into this world

And I will love you into the next.

I am the moon's light shimmering on the sea.

I am a cat sleeping by the fire

And a deer grazing in the forest.

I am the bear overcoming his prey

And the dark chill of night.

I am the Cailleach, the hag, the most feared and the least called.

I am the Goddess of prunes and old bones.

I am a crow.

I am the one-eyed Goddess with a frost apron who sees all things.

There are times when I am beautiful to behold

And others when I am the ugliest creature of all.

When I will it, I am irresistible to men.

They've all had me, each in their own way.

I love a man or woman between my thighs.

Priests have visited me and I welcome them too

Although often they flee

At least for a while.

They always return white haired and wise

To humbly lay their heads in my frost apron.

I create storms for my forests

And wind for the crows.

I am the sleep that heals.

I am the source of all life.

I can make you whole again

And give you new life.

I am dry twigs that snap.

I am a great drought.

I am the pouring rain

And the hurricane that floods fields.

I am the darkness and the light.

I am the food in your hearth,

The fire beneath your pots.

I am your baby's gurgle.

I am life that constantly renews.

I am health and illness,

Death and life.

I am loneliness and despair,

And the greatest bliss.

There is nothing and no one

I cannot embrace.

I am the Cailleach

The Grandmother of all things.

Appendix I
Pantheon of Celtic Divinities

Pantheon of Irish Divinities

Ernmas (Creator Goddess): mother of Danu and the triple Goddesses of Ireland: Eriu, Banbha, and Fodhla.

Danu: mother of the tribe, the Tuatha Dé Danann.

Danu & the Sun God, Bilé: parents of the Dagda.

Dagda: son/husband of Danu; father of Brighid and Aine, also Lugh, Ogma and Aengus Og.

Brighid: daughter of the Dagda; mother of Ruadan.

Aine: daughter of the Dagda, wife of mortal Codal, then Mannan Mac Lir.

Sea God, Lir: father of sea deity, Manannan Mac Lir.

Manannan Mac Lir: father of Fand and consort of Aine.

Aengus Og: beloved of the faery Caer Ibormeith.

Caer Ibormeith: daughter of Prince Ethal Anbuail of the Sidhe.

Concobar Mac Nessa: brother of Dechtire, uncle of Cuchulain.

Cathbad, the Druid: father of Dechtire.

Dechtire and Lugh: parents of Setanta, who became the hero Cuchulain.

Forgall Monach: father of Emer.

Cuchulain: husband of Emer, hero of Ireland.

Emer: wife of Cuchulain.

Pantheon of Scottish/Irish Divinities

Scatach and Cuchulain: parents of Connal (Scottish-Irish union).

Brighid/Brigid: (appears throughout the Celtic lands).

Cailleach: Self Made.

Scatach: warrior woman of Skye and Cuchulain's teacher/lover.

Aoife: the sister, twin or other aspect of Scatach.

Connal: son of Scatach and Cuchulain.

Uathach: daughter of Scatach.

Biblical Characters

Noah: grandfather of Ceasair.

Ceasair: the granddaughter of Noah.

Fintan: the husband of Ceasair.

Appendix II
Lebor Gabala Erenn's
Six Invasions of Ireland

The *Lebor Gabala Erenn* or the *Book of the Taking of Ireland* is a collection of poetry and prose that records six tribes that invaded Ireland. The first four groups were said to die or be washed away by floods. The recorded years of the invasions vary widely and are generally regarded as a pseudo-history or as myth. It may be that the monks wanted to link the Irish to Jesus. Then again, there may be an ancient link to the lineage of David. The Hero or Heroine's journey is filled with mystery. Recent scientific research is discovering that there was a red-headed race that lived about the time of the Tuatha Dé Danann.

2958 B.C. — The first Invasion of the People of Ceasair, grand-daughter of Noah, land at Dún na mBarc, now known as Bantry Bay located in Co Cork in the south of Ireland.

2658 B.C. — The second Invasion by the Muintir Partholóin or the people of Parthalán who arrived 300 years after Ceasair (also spelled Cessair). They are agricultural people who were said to die in a plague.

2350 B.C. — The third Invasion by the Nemedians, who arrived after their Parthalán predecessors. The Nemedians also die or are forced to leave the island.

1934 B.C. — The fourth Invasion by the Fir Bolgs (ancestors of the Nemedians who had settled in Greece and then returned to an uninhabited Ireland). They are shepherds and agriculturalists who lived peacefully until the arrival of the Tuatha Dé Danann. The last High King of the Fir Bolgs, Eochaid mac Eirc (married to the Goddess Tailtiu) was believed to be the example of a perfect king. Nuada, king of the Tuatha De Danann, challenged Eochaid mac Eirc's leadership. In some tales, the Fir Bolgs fled Ireland; in others, they retreated to Connacht in the west of Ireland.

1897 B.C. until 1700 B.C. — The fifth invasion by the tribe of Danu, the Tuatha Dé (Tuatha Dé Danann). These people were tall with red or blonde hair, blue or green eyes, and pale skin. Poets say the Tuatha Dé were a race of God-like people who were gifted with supernatural powers and that they came from four mythical Northern cities: Murias, Gorias, Falias, and Finias, which some scholars place in Lochlann (Norway). Other mystics claim that the Tuatha Dé were from the sunken continent of Atlantis, for they came from the lands under the wave. One of their Otherworldly dimensions is known as Tir Na n-og, or The Land of Eternal Youth; another is Tir Na Ban, the Land of Women. In order to reach these worlds, the seeker must pass through the gateways of the Sidhe mounds, where the veil between the worlds is thin, and therefore easier to travel through. Time was different in these places, for in the

Otherworld, time stands still, while it passes quickly in the land of mortals. Mythologists claim that this magical race became the Pagan Gods of Ireland.

1700 B.C. — The sixth Invasion by the Milesians, Gaels who sailed to Ireland from Iberia (now known as the Iberian Peninsula that is divided between the countries of Spain, Portugal, and Andorra). These people of largely Spanish decent are thought by some scholars to be the race that settled Ireland. Other researchers disagree and say that the Irish arose out of the soil of their own land. The Tuatha Dé and the Milesians agreed to divide Ireland between them, but in an unusual way. The Milesians took the surface Earth, while the Tuatha Dé claimed the underworld or Otherworld. Poets and mystics might say that they share Ireland, but in different dimensions. They may still inhabit Ireland.

Appendix III
A Goddess Timeline and Thealogy: Her-story

Pre-History — Mystics describe a Golden Age that existed where deities, nature spirits, elves, and dwarfs existed before the emergence of human beings.

33,000 BC to 394 AD — Thealogists[1] claim that the Great Goddess was worshipped as a monotheistic deity during this period of time.

26,000 to 19,000 years ago, thick ice sheets covered Ireland and Britain. During the Ice Age, and later, as warmth returned to the land, the Great Mother was honored as the Giver of Life and Keeper of the Hearth. She symbolized fertility and the life-supportive nature of the feminine. The Hearth Keeper tradition was passed on through Greek Hestia, Roman Vesta, and to her priestesses, the Vestal Virgins, whose job was to keep sacred fires burning. The fires were extinguished in 394 AD.

---

1 Thealogy comes from the Greek "thea" meaning Goddess, as opposed to "theo" meaning God. It is a term used when studying from a feminist perspective. Thealogians come from many backgrounds including Christianity, Judaism, Buddhism, Paganism and Neo-Paganism.

24,000 to 22,000 BCE — Voluptuous statues were carved to represent the Mother Goddess. The most famous is now known as the Venus of Willendorf.

10,000 BCE — Stone Age figures were carved in honor of the Mother Goddess.

8000 to 4000 BCE — Mesolithic hunter-gatherers settle in Ireland. The Spirit of the Hearth takes on the form of a clever old woman. In Ireland and Scotland she is known as the Cailleach.

6500 to 3500 BCE — According to Scholar Marija Gimbutas, a Goddess-centered culture existed in Old Europe. Clay, stone, and ivory statues of women were carved suggesting that women were honored and that there may have been a "matrilineage" society, in which kinship is traced through the female lineage.

4000 to 2500 BCE — Temples in the Scottish Orkney Islands show large Mother-Goddess figures, leading scholars to believe that the divine creative force was primarily regarded as feminine.

3600 to 2500 — Mnajdra and Hagar Qim, two Earth-Mother Stone temples in Malta, were built in the form of a voluptuous woman or Goddess's body.

2958 B.C. — According to the *Labor Gabala*, Ceasair arrives on Ireland's shores.

1897 B.C. until 1700 B.C. — The tribe of Danu, the Tuatha Dé (Tuatha Dé Danann), thrive in Ireland. The gods and goddesses of the Celtic Pantheon emerge, including: Eriu, Fodhla, and Banba (the three early Goddesses of Ireland), Aine, Brigit (Triple Goddess Brigid or the more ancient Goddess Brighid), Angus (Aengus), and Caer Ibormeith.

800 to 50 BCE — Celtic polytheism was the practice of the Iron Age people of Western Europe. Polytheistic pagan religions thrived during this period. The Celtics did not write down their myths, so for Celtic folklore we largely depend on the stories recorded by monks.

43 BCE Romanization of Celtic Stories: Danu becomes Demeter.

1 BC — Scatach, Emer and Cuchulain from the Ulster Cycle live in this century.

1st–4th Century AD — Gnostics worshipped Sophia, the Goddess of Wisdom. Gnosis is a feminine noun meaning knowledge.

325 AD — Council of Nicaea and the formation of the Roman Catholic Church.

341 — AD Emperor decrees all pagan worship illegal.

394 — AD The College of the Vestal Virgins was disbanded and the fires put out by the Christian Emperor Theodosius I.

450 AD — The snakes of Ireland were killed during the last Ice Age, but the symbol of the snake refers to Goddess related religions. It was during this time that St Patrick drove the Goddesses traditions, the Druids and the polytheistic religions from Ireland. He was not nearly as brutal as the Inquisition, and many myths and legends survive because the Christian monks recorded them.

451 AD — The Goddess Brighid becomes St Brigit.

5th century AD — The Irish became literate and their ancient writing system (known as Ogham) was replaced with Latin.

700 AD — Stories about Cuchulain and Emer were recorded in the Ulster Tales.

785–1750 AD — The Catholic Church decreed at the Council of Paderborn, that Witchcraft was punishable by death. Until the 18th century European and American women and some men were tortured for being witches, healers, seers, midwives, visionaries, unusual, rebels, or holding financial or other types of power. For a thousand years unknown numbers of women, ranging from 60,000 to 9 million women were tortured, burned and/or killed as witches.

800 AD — *The Book of Kells* is created preserving Celtic imagery, knots and early Christian symbolism.

9th Century — The illuminated *Book of Armagh* written mainly in Latin is published, preserving the story of St Patrick and other important Irish folklore.

12th Century — British rule of Ireland lasts until 1921.

13th Century — The English language is introduced to Ireland following the Norman Conquest.

Middle Ages — Celtic practices became extinct and were replaced by Christian practices.

16th Century — Queen Elizabeth I of England encouraged the immigration of Scottish Protestants. The Anglo-Irish minority dominated the Irish Catholics.

16th-17th Centuries — Plantations of Ireland continued, in which English Protestants confiscated land from the older Catholic ruling class.

1752 — The British Empire adopts the Gregorian calendar.

18th Century — Dublin was the home of an Irish-language literary circle and although few were literate, women were of great importance in the oral tradition.

1840 — Potato blight caused one million to starve to death and two million people to immigrate to the United States.

1886-1953 — Maud Gonne, an English born Irish revolutionary of Anglo-Irish heritage, served as W.B Yeats' muse and inspiration. Her husband, John MacBride, was executed with the other leaders of the Easter Uprising.

1916 — The Easter Uprising or Easter Rebellion was an uprising against British rule. The Irish were crushed and the leaders were executed. However, the Irish Republican Army (IRA) launched a campaign against British forces that was eventually to succeed.

1918-1922 — Irish and American women are given the right to vote.

1919-1921 — Irish War of Independence.

1921 — Anglo-Irish treaty *(An Conradh Angla-Eireannach)* is signed between Ireland and Britain.

1922 — Establishment of the Irish free state in which southern Ireland becomes a sovereign and self ruling county. The northern counties of Ireland chose to remain part of the United Kingdom.

19th and 20th Century Irish Literary Renaissance, also known as Celtic Twilight, supported a flowering of literary talent and re-telling of folklore and myth. Irish Gaelic was restored as the national language.

1889 — W.B Yeats' *The Wanderings of Oisin and Other Poems* is published based on the lyrics of the Fenian Cycle of Irish mythology.

1897 — Lady Gregory co-founds the Irish Literary Theatre with W.B Yeats, George Moore and Edward Martyn.

1899 — W.B. Yeats' poem "The Song of Wandering Aengus" is published in his book *The Wind Among The Reeds*.

1904 — Opening of the Abbey Theatre, a national theatre for Ireland which performed plays by Irish authors.

1979 — An international treaty and international bill equal of rights for women, "Convention on the Elimination of All Forms of Discrimination against Women" or CEDAW, was adopted by the United Nations General Assembly. It came into force on 3 September 1981.

1974–1991 — Marija Gimbutas publishes three books: *The Goddesses and Gods of Old Europe, The Language of the Goddess* and *The Civilization of the Goddess,* comparing and contrasting a Goddess or gynocentric (woman-centered) system, with the patriarchal Bronze Age culture that replaced it. She described the gynocentric cultures as peaceful, in which women were honored and enjoyed economic equality.

1970 — Neo-Pagan Goddess Movement arises in reaction to male dominated religious orders in which the Goddess is considered a personal guardian.

1979 — Naomi Goldenberg in her book *The Changing of the Gods,* popularizes the feminist term "thealogy."

1980s — A feminine tradition of Wicca known as Dianic Wicca is started by Zsuzsanna Budapest who wrote, *The Holy Book of Women's Mysteries.*

1984 — Jean Shinoda Bolen publishes the wildly successful *Goddess in Every Woman*, inviting women to identify their inner Goddess.

2012 — The Mayan elders state that the old paradigm has ended and a new age has begun with the return of the divine feminine (the Goddess) on earth.

2017 — The missing stories of the Goddesses re-emerge.

Appendix IV
Calendar of the Goddess:
Balanced Sun & Moon

In order to move back into harmony with Nature, we can observe the intelligent patterns of the natural world and how they support our health and well-being. We can learn to respond intuitively to the energies that live in each season, by walking on the land and observing the life-affirming patterns of the sun and moon. The earth-based religions honor the sun and the moon in a calendar with eight wheels, or times of celebration.

1st **WHEEL: Samhain (October 31–November 2):** The reign of the Winter Queen, the Cailleach, begins at this time. Samhain marks the end and the beginning of the Celtic calendar. It is known as the turning of the 1st Wheel. On these three days, the veils between our world and the Otherworlds are thin. It is a time to honor our ancestors and guardians who have supported us throughout our lives. Caer and Aengus Og can be celebrated during this time as guardians who teach us how to slip between parallel dimensions.

2nd **WHEEL: Winter Solstice/Yule (Dec 20-22):** The Cailleach is traditionally honored during the Winter Solstice, the shortest day of the year. Death and rebirth are honored during the turning of the 2nd Wheel. The darkness of winter is cast off and the promise of spring and summer returns. A Yule log is prepared with leaves, along with messages of what is outdated, and families gather to invite in the Light of the new sun.

3rd WHEEL: Imbolc (February 1-2): The return of light and life is celebrated during the 3rd Turning of the Wheel. Imbolc marks the ending of winter when lambs are born and the first flowers begin to appear in Ireland. Fires are lit to awaken the Goddess Brighid; stories are told and flowers are planted in her honor.

4th WHEEL: Spring Equinox/Eostre (March 20-22): Also known as *Alban Eilir* or Light of the Earth, the Spring Equinox marks the 4th Turning of the Wheel and the beginning of spring in full bloom. Days and nights are balanced; energies are at their peak. The union of the Green Man and Mother Earth is honored with seeds planted in prepared soil. Ancient Europeans also worshipped the Great Mother Goddess Eostre at this time or later in April. Her symbol was the fertile rabbit or hare, and in some legends, she could shape-shift into a hare. Hens lay many eggs during spring and have been used for centuries to celebrate fertility and life. Eostre Eggs are often painted red in honor of the joyful Mother Goddess.

5th WHEEL: May Day/Beltane (April 30-May 1): Beltane officially begins at moonrise on April 30, and it marks the second half of the Celtic year and the 5th Turning of the Wheel. Fires were traditionally lit in honor of Belenos or Bilé (the Celtic God of the Sun) and the May Queen Danu. Once dances took place in stone circles to activate the energies of the landscape. May 1 is a day when ritual dancing is performed all over the western world in honor of the May King and Queen.

6TH WHEEL: Summer Solstice/Litha (June 20-22): Summer Solstice was witnessed as a time in which the sun stood still. Celts would light fires to add to the energy of the sun (honored as an intelligent life-sustaining force) so it could continue its cycle. The longest day of the year – celebrated as the Summer Solstice, Litha, Midsummer, and *Alban Hefin* or the Light of the Shore – occurs at midsummer between June 20-22. The Summer Solstice marks the **6th Turning of the Wheel**. The Solar Goddess **Aine** is celebrated at this time, and in some legends, she crowns the Summer King.

7th WHEEL: Lughnasa/Lammas (July 31-Aug 1): Lughnasa means the games of Lugh. In myth and legend, it is said that the Goddess Taillte once resided on the magical *Temair* (Hill of Tara). In ancient Ireland, she was known as the foster-mother of the Light, who took the embodied form as the Sun God, Lugh. Upon her death, she requested that games be held each year in her honor on the lands she had cleared. Lugh held the first games, which were rather like an early Irish Olympics. There was also music, feasting and story-telling. Today many people make a meal to celebrate the harvest and the feminine energy that sustains us.

8th WHEEL: Autumn Equinox/Mabon (September 21-22): Mabon is a time to rest after the harvest, and it is symbolized by the Cornucopia or the Horn of Plenty – both a masculine and feminine symbol. Like the Spring Equinox, the days and nights are equally balanced. It marks the turning of the **8th Wheel**, and this is a time to give thanks to the goodness of the Great Goddess who nourishes us.

NO TIME: Samhain (October 31- November 1): This date marks
the end of the Celtic Year. It is at this time, when the veils are thin,
that we can give thanks to our ancestors and also contemplate the
mysteries. The space between October 31 and November 1st can be
called "No Time." Mystics contemplate the unknown during this
period, and some initiates may practice slipping between the veils
into the Otherworlds. On November 1, the wheel turns and we
continue to explore the cyclical nature of existence as the light of the
sun wanes. Brighid goes to sleep, and on November 1, the Cailleach
begins her reign as the Queen of Winter.

Glossary
Guide to Pronunciation & Terms

Aengus Og: Celtic God of Love, Beauty, and Poetry, who fell in love with Caer Ibormeith.

Aine (Irish pronunciation "AAN-yuh" or "AW-neh"): an Irish Solar Goddess.

Anu (also known as "Danu" or "Don" or "Anand"): an Irish Mother-Goddess or Celtic Goddess of Fertility. In some tales, she was the wife of the Sun God, Belenos and the Mother of the Tuatha Dé Danann. With Danu and Aine, she was absorbed into Christianity as St. Anne and may have been demonized as Black Annis by those who wished to destroy Goddess worship. Mystics say Anu still observes us from afar, looking down on us from the night's sky, where she appears as *Llys Don*, also known as the constellation of Casseopeia.

Aoife (Irish pronunciation "Eefa"): the sister, rival, or good half of the Scottish warrior woman Goddess, Scatach.

Badb (Irish pronunciation "Bibe," similar to bribe): means crow. She is one of the three Goddesses, with Macha and Nemain (or Anand), that form the triple Goddess of War known as the Morrigan.

Banba or **Banbha** (Irish pronunciation "BAN uh va"): daughter of the Tuatha Dé Danann and one of the triple Goddesses who protects Ireland, along with Eriu and Fodhla.

Belenos: Irish solar divinity and husband of Anu.

Beltane: The Celtic May Day, beginning on moonrise on May Day Eve, is generally celebrated on May 1. The Spring fertility festival honors the solar divinity Belenos and his union with the May Queen. Weddings and hand-fastings are common at this time. It is often celebrated with May Pole dancing and jumping the Beltane fires for luck.

Bilé: meaning "sacred tree" is the Celtic God of Light and Healing; the husband of Danu and father of the Dagda.

Boann or Boand: created the Boyne River from the Well of Wisdom and is celebrated as a Goddess of poetry, white cows and wisdom. She is the wife of Nechtan, a water God.

Brighid (Gaelic pronunciation "breed"), also **Brigid, Brigit, or Bride**: Irish Goddess of fire who was absorbed into Celtic Christianity as St. Brigit. Brighid was known as the daughter of the Dagda and was born with rays of sun beaming from her head. As a solar Goddess, her gifts were knowledge, inspiration, and healing. Since she is a master herbalist, she is often invoked during childbirth. Brighid is the Irish muse of poetry and song. She is also known as Mary of the Gael.

Brigit of Kildare: an early Christian abbess and saint who died in 525 CE. Brigit the Saint possessed much of the magic and healing powers of the Goddess Brighid or Bride.

Bru na Boinne: (Irish pronunciation "brew nah bonyah"): a place in Co. Louth known as the bend in the River Boyne. It is associated with the Sidhe and is thought to be a portal to Otherworld.

Ancient megalithic structures are found at Bru na Boinne including Newgrange, Knowth and Dowth. In folklore, it is the place where Angus and Caer Ibormeith dwell.

Caer (pronounced "Keer"): Caer Ibormeith, who every other year turned into a swan for a year. She was the beloved of Angus.

Cailleach (Gaelic pronunciation "KAL-y-ach" or "Coy-luck"): a name meaning "veiled one." Cailleach is an ancient ancestor deity or Hag Goddess who appears in Scottish, Irish, and Manx mythologies. She is often described as an aspect of winter or as an old woman. Brighid is her spring/summer counterpart. Her reign begins at Samhain (October 31 or November 1) and lasts through the winter months.

Cathbad (Irish pronunciation "kath-bad"): King Conchobar's powerful Druid from the Ulster Cycle of mythology. He married Maga and fathered three daughers including Dechtire, the mother of Cuchulain. He was highly respected at the court of Emain Macha and educated many in the arts of magic, law and war.

Ceasair: (two pronunciations: "KAH-seer" or "Sea-sayer"): the granddaughter of Noah.

Codal: husband of Aine and chieftain in the lineage of Danu.

Conchobar Mac Nessa (Irish pronunciation "CON-or mic NESH-ah"): the Celtic King of Ulster around the time of Jesus Christ. He is the son of Ness and Cathbad the Druid, and Cuchulain's uncle.

Connal: son of Scatach and Cuchulain.

Cuchulain (Irish pronunciation "Koo-hull-in") **of Muirthemne**: a great Irish Hero from Ulster, who married Emer.

Dagda: the God of Goodness, Abundance, and Fertility. Rather like the Judeo-Christian story in which Eve is taken from the rib of

Adam, the Dagda emerges out of Danu to become her husband and lover. He is the father of Aine, Brighid, Lugh, Ogma, Aengus Og and other children of the Tuatha Dé Danann.

Danu (see "Anu" and "Don"): Irish Goddess, known as the Mother of the Tuatha Dé Danann.

Dechtire (pronounced "dek-tyre"): the daughter of the Goddess Maga and Cathbad, the Druid; mother of Cuchulain; half-sister of King Conchobar Mac Nessa.

deva: a nature spirit or spiritual force within nature.

Don: Welsh Mother Goddess, who is known in Ireland as Danu or Anu.

Druids: the educated poets, healers, leaders, and often magical men and women of the ancient Celts.

Dub Sainglend (Irish pronunciation "dub-sane-glend"): one of Cuchulain's two warhorses that pulled his chariot into battle. Also known as the "Black of Saingliu," this great horse was a gift from either Macha or the Morrigan.

Emer (Irish pronunciation "EE-mer" or "EM-er"): the Irish paragon of beauty and the wife of Cuchulain.

Eostre: Ancient Europeans worshipped the Great Mother Goddess Eostre during the Spring Equinox (March 21) or later in April. Her symbol was the fertile rabbit or hare, and in some legends, she could shape-shift into a hare.

Eochaid mac Eirc: (Irish pronunciation "Owen mack Eark") the last High King of the Fir Bolgs, Eochaid mac Eirc was considered to be the example of a perfect king. He was eventually defeated by the Triple War Goddess, the Morrigan or Morigú.

Eriu (Irish pronunciation "EYHR-yoo"): one of the triple Goddesses who protects Ireland, along with Banbha and Fodhla. She eventually became the personification of Ireland.

Ethal Anbuail: a prince of the Sidhe and father of Caer Ibormeith.

Fand: a faery who appears as an Otherworldly sea bird. After being wounded by him, she becomes the lover of the Hero Cuchulain. In some legends, she is the wife of Manannan Mac Lir, who shakes a cloak of forgetfulness between the pair.

Flidais: the wife of Ailill Finn and the lover of Fergus. Flidais was one of the Tuatha Dé Danann and was known for her beautiful hair. Flidais drove through forests in a chariot pulled by deer and owned a special cow that gave plentiful milk.

Fintan/Fintain mac Bochra: an Irish poet and seer. Fintan was one of the three men or demi-gods that sailed on the ship or ark with Ceasair, the granddaughter of Noah. His sixteen wives, included Ceasair. In folklore, in order to survive during the flood he transformed himself into a salmon, then an eagle, and a hawk, before resuming his human form. He lived for 5,500 years and, because he could shape-shift, he was referred to as "The Wise." He is linked to the Fenian Cycle of Irish Mythology and the stories of the Salmon of Knowledge or Wisdom.

Fodhla/Fodla (Irish pronunciation "Fóla"): one of the triple Goddesses who protects Ireland, along with Banbha and Eriu.

Forgall Monach (Irish pronunciation "for-gal mon-ak"): appears in the Ulster Cycle as the wily father of Emer. He rules as a king or chieftain and lives at a fortress known as Luglochta Loga, the Gardens of Lugh, in Lusk, Co Dublin.

Fomorians: a supernatural race from Irish mythology, often described as gods of the more destructive aspects of nature. They were said to come from beneath the ground or sea and are often portrayed as hostile. They were Ireland's first settlers and were often at odds with the Tuatha Dé Danann. They are sometimes linked to the gods of Norse mythology.

geis or geas: in Irish and Welsh mythology, this is an idiosyncratic taboo, curse, spell, obligation, or prohibition placed upon someone. *Geiss* in Old Irish means 'swan.'

glefiosa (pronounced in Welsh *glay fee'sa*): our bright inner knowing or gnosis.

Grian (Irish pronunciation "green"): means sun. A pre-Christian Irish Goddess.

Imbolc (Gaelic pronunciation "IM-bulk" or "ee-Molk"): also known as Candlemas or Bride's Day, an ancient ceremony held on February 1 or 2 of each year in honor the Goddess Brighid. It is one of the four Celtic fire ceremonies and marks the passage of winter into spring. Imbolc honors the phases of the triple Goddess: maiden, mother, and crone.

keening: Irish ritual invented by the Goddess Brighid to mourn the dead.

Ladra: Ceasair's navigator.

Laeg (Irish pronunciation "leg"): charioteer of Cuchulain.

Lair Derg: Aine's fast red mare.

Lammas (also known as Lughnasa): an Irish Gaelic name for the games of Lugh, the Celtic God of Light. It was an early Christian festival, held on August 1, celebrating the fruits of harvest. Often, loaves of bread were taken to church and laid on the altar. The Greek Goddesses Demeter and Ceres are also honored at this time.

***Lebor Gabala Erenn* or *Book of Invasions of Ireland*:** the earliest known history written by the Irish. It is in the public domain. Some scholars say the book was developed over centuries while others claim it was compiled in the 11th century. It is now generally regarded as myth.

Liath Macha (Irish pronunciation "Lee-ath mock-uh"): Cuchulain's horse, meaning "grey of Macha."

Litha: also known as Midsummer or Summer Solstice, it is a holiday celebrated annually around June 21, the longest day of the year. It is considered the most powerful day for both the sun's and the Sun God's or Goddess's full power. Fires are ritually burned to drive harmful influences from the land. Aine is celebrated on this day.

Lugaid mac Noís (Irish pronunciation "lugh-guide mak noise"): a king of Munster and suitor of Emer.

Lugh (Irish pronunciation "Loo"): Irish High King of the distant past. His Welsh counterpart is Lleu Llaw Gyffes.

Lughnasa (also known as Lammas): named after the sun god, Lugh. A holiday celebrated August 1, which marked the ending of the Celtic year. Lughnasa was the last of the four great feasts (the Celtic year begins with Samhain on October 31/November 1). In Ireland, it is said that Lugh created the festival in honor of his mother, the Goddess Tailtui.

Mabon (also known as Fall Equinox or Harvest Tide): The Celtic festival of mid-harvest, celebrated on the Autumn Equinox, around September 21.

Macha (Irish pronunciation "MOCK-uh"): Goddess of Ancient Ireland.

Mag Mell: the Irish mythical realm, which was achieved through a glorious death. It was generally thought to exist beneath the sea. The ruler is often Manannan Mac Lir, a Celtic sea deity.

Manannan Mac Lir: a sea deity in Celtic mythology who drove a chariot through the waves. He is associated with both the

Tuatha Dé Danann and the Fomorians. The Isle of Man is named after him.

Morrigan or Morigú: Irish triple Goddess of war, combining Macha, Badb, and Nemain (or Anand). The term may arise from the Old English "maere" meaning nightmare. She is mentioned in the *Lebor Gabala Erenn* as one of the Tuatha Dé Danann, daughter of the Creator Goddess Ernmas, or Danu. She may be linked in Arthurian legend to Morgan le Fay, sister of King Arthur.

Nemain: the frenzied nature of war; often part of the triple Goddess of War, the Morrigan.

Ogma: the Celtic god of writing and creator of the Ogham alphabet.

Ostara (Spring Equinox): the original Easter, when eggs are painted and flowers are gathered. It is celebrated around March 21.

Paps of Danu: Irish mythological site near Cork in the southwest province of Munster. These are two identical rounded hills, each crowned with a rock construction known as a cairn.

Ruadan: son of King Bres and Brigid, he was killed during battle. Brigid grieved so much that she invented keening, a form of lamenting for the dead.

Salmon of Wisdom/Salmon of Knowledge: (in Irish "*bradán feasa*") is from the Fenian Cycle of Irish Mythology. A salmon ate nine hazelnuts that fell into the Well of Wisdom and gained realization of all the knowledge of the world. The poet Finegas caught the fish, but while cooking the wisdom passed to Fionn, who became the wise leader of the Fianna.

Samhain (Gaelic pronunciation "Sah-win." Some Irish speakers say "Shavnah"): Halloween, All Hallow's Eve, or Samhain is celebrated around October 31. Marking the end of the Celtic year, it is a time to honor the ancestors and think of those who have passed away.

Scatach (Gaelic pronunciation "sca-hah" or "skya"): a Scottish warrior Goddess.

Sidhe (Irish pronunciation "Shee"): the tall, beautiful people of myth and legend.

sylph: an elemental being connected with air, often called a Faery.

Summer Solstice: see Litha.

Taoiseach: a chieftan or leader.

Tara (The Hill of Tara or "Cnoc na Teamhrach"): is located near the River Boyne in Co Meath, Ireland. According to tradition, it is the seat of the High King of Ireland.

Thealogy: comes from the Greek "thea" meaning Goddess, as opposed to "theo" meaning God. It is a term used when studying from a feminist perspective. Thealogians come from many backgrounds including Christianity, Judaism, Buddhism, Paganism and Neo-Paganism.

Tir Na Ban: (Irish pronunciation "Thi/r na Ban"): a legendary Otherworldly land of women.

Tir Na n-og or **Tir-Nan-Og:** (Irish pronunciation "Thi/r na nOg"): Land of Eternal Youth.

Tuatha Dé Danann (Irish pronunciation "Too- a-ha-dae Donnan") or simply the **Tuatha:** the tribe of the Goddess Danu, a supernatural race in Irish Mythology.

Uathach (Irish pronunciation "You-ath-ache"): the daughter of Scatach and niece of Aoife.

undines: elemental beings associated with water.

Undry (*Coire Unsic* in Irish): the Dagda's Cauldron of Abundance from which no person ever left unsatisfied. It is thought to be an early expression of the Grail.

Winter Solstice: see Yule.

Yggdrasil (pronounced "egg-dra-sail"): a Norse evergreen Ash, known in Scandinavian Mythology as the World Tree that holds earth, heaven, and hell in its roots and branches.

Yule: arising out of the Anglo-Saxon word "Iul," — it means wheel. It is a celebration of the Wheel of Life. Yule is observed on the Winter Solstice, around December 21, the shortest day of the year. One of the four Fire Ceremonies of the Celts, it is hailed as the time when the Goddess becomes the Great Mother and gives birth to the Sun King. Yule was absorbed into Christianity as Christmas. Mystics know that in the darkest of times, it is wise to seek a spark of hope and the return of light.

Bibliography
A Celtic Mythology Library

Adams, Hazard. *Lady Gregory,* Bucknell University Press & Associated University Presses, London, UK, 1973.

Blair, Nancy. *The Book of Goddesses,* Vega, London, UK, 2002.

Bolen, Jean Shinoda, MD. *Goddesses in Everywoman: Powerful Archetypes in Women's Lives,* Harper Perennial, New York, NY, 1984.

Bonheim, Jalaja, editor. *Goddess: A Celebration in Art and Literature,* Stewart, Tabori & Chang: New York, 1997.

Caldecott, Morya. *Women in Celtic Myth,* Arrow Books, London, UK, 1988.

Campbell, Joseph. *Goddesses: Mysteries of the Feminine Divine,* New World Library,
Novato, California, 2013.

Cates, Ayn Wesley. *Disguise, Deceit and the Divine Spokesperson: A Study of Lady Gregory's Plays,* Doctoral Thesis approved by King's College London, April 1993. (Interlibrary Loan: Senate House, London, UK)

Downing, Christine. *Women's Mysteries, Toward a Poetics of Gender,* Spring Journal, Inc., New Orleans, LA, 2003.

Ellis, Peter Berresford. *The Druids,* William B. Eerdman's Publishing Co., Grand Rapids, MI, 1994.

Gimbutas, Marija. *The Goddesses and Gods of Old Europe, Myths and Cult Images,* University of California Press, Berkeley and Los Angeles, CA, 2007.

Gimbutas, Marija. *The Living Goddesses,* University of California Press, Berkeley and Los Angeles, CA, 1999.

Graves, Robert. *The White Goddess: A Historical Grammar of Poetic Myth,* Farrar, Straus and Giroux, New York, NY, 2013.

Gregory, Lady. *Cuchulain of Muirthemne,* Colin Smythe, Gerrards Cross, Buckinghamshire, UK, 1905/1973.

Gregory, Lady. *Gods and Fighting Men,* Colin Smythe, Gerrards Cross, Buckinghamshire, UK, 1905/1970.

Heaney, Marie. *Over Nine Waves: A Book of Irish Legends,* Faber & Faber, Inc., London, UK, 1995.

Hidalgo, Sharlyn. *The Healing Power of Trees,* Llewellyn Publications, Woodbury, Minnesota, 2015.

Jones, Kathy. *Spinning the Wheel of Ana: A Spiritual Quest to Find the British Primal Ancestors,* Ariadne Publications, Glastonbury, UK, 1994.

Leviton, Richard. *Encyclopedia of Earth Myths,* Hampton Road Publishing, Charlottesville, VA, 2005.

Loomis, Roger Sherman. *The Grail: From Celtic Myth to Christian Symbol,* Constable and Company Limited, London, UK, 1992.

Macalister, Robert Alexander Stewart. *Lebor Gabala Erenn: The book of the taking of Ireland, Volume 1,* Hardpress Publishing, Miami, FL, 1938.

Markale, Jean. *Women of the Celts,* Inner Traditions, Rochester, VT, 1972.